THE
VATICAN
PIMPERNEL

The Wartime Exploits of
Monsignor Hugh O'Flaherty

Brian Fleming

The Collins Press

Published in 2008 by
The Collins Press
West Link Park
Doughcloyne
Wilton
Cork

British Cataloguing in Publication data

Fleming, Brian
    The Vatican pimpernel : the wartime exploits of
    Monsignor O'Flaherty
    1. O'Flaherty, Hugh 2. Catholic Church - Clergy -
    Biography 3. Priests - Ireland - Biography 4.
    Diplomats - Vatican City - Biography 5. Escapes -
    Italy - History - 20th century 6. World War, 1939-
    1945 - Underground movements - Italy
    I. Title
    940.5'486'092

ISBN-13: 9781905172573

Typeset by The Collins Press
Typeset in Berkeley Book 11pt
Printed by GraphyCems, Spain

For Aedín, Conor, Ronan, Kevin, Aoife, Ciara and the wonderful Mary who brought them all into my life.

Contents

Acknowledgements

A wide range of people were of assistance to me in writing this book. Some helped by way of provision of information, or a suggestion as to where that information might be found, others by words of encouragement. My sincere thanks are due to: Kathleen Wilde, Fergus Fleming, Cardinal Seán Brady, Eamonn and Ann Fleming, Monsignor John Hanly, Gerry Jeffers, Vincent and Margaret Lennon, Frank Lewis, John McHugh, Archbishop Diarmuid Martin, Eimear Millsopp, Michael Moynihan TD, Maurice O'Keeffe, Tony O'Keeffe, Barbara O'Toole, Aideen Overton, Fionnuala Watters, Sinéad Allart in Cherbourg, Eman Bonnici in Malta, Bishop Brian Farrell and Monsignor Charles Burns in Rome, John Mallon in London and Billy Vincent in Monaco.

During the course of my research I received great assistance from: the staff of the Berkeley Library in Trinity College Dublin, Siobhán McCrystal and Mary Roche in Palmerstown Library, Noreen Sullivan and Barthy Flynn in Cahersiveen Library, the staff of the National Archives, Dublin, and their counterparts in the National Archives of the United Kingdom, London, Maureen Sweeney of the Archives Section, Department of Foreign Affairs, Séamus Helferty and his colleagues in the Archives section, James Joyce Library at University College Dublin, Bozenna Rotman of Yad Vashem, Jerusalem, and staff of the British, Canadian and Israeli Embassies in Dublin and the British Embassy to the Holy See in Rome.

I would like to express my particular gratitude to those who gave permission for me to use extracts from books and archival material: to Mrs Kathleen MacWhite in relation to her late father-in-law's wonderful archive, to Dr Brendan Kennelly for his poem, to Will Derry in Nottinghamshire in relation to his late father's book and to William Simpson and Pen and Sword Books in respect of *A Vatican Lifeline '44*. I would like to thank the following who have kindly given permission to reproduce photographs in this book: Will Derry, William Simpson and Pen and Sword Books, and the Provincial of the Capuchin Order. Jim Butler and his colleagues in Repro 35, Dublin, were very skilful in reproducing these photographs. Every effort has been made to trace all copyright holders, although the passage of time since most sources were published meant I was not always successful. Any omissions are entirely unintentional and regretted. The publisher will be happy to hear from copyright holders not acknowledged and undertakes to rectify any errors or omissions in future editions.

Part of the joy of writing this book has been the opportunity it gave me to meet some of the Monsignor's family and friends. I had hugely enjoyable and interesting conversations with Dr Veronica Dunne in Dublin and Danny O'Connor in Cahersiveen. Throughout the whole process the Monsignor's nephew, Hugh O'Flaherty, has been extremely helpful, particularly in relation to making available family archival material. No request for information or clarification was too much trouble and his response was invariably both speedy and enlightening. Time was never an issue and indeed he and I spent a most enjoyable day in the company of the local Dáil Deputy, Michael Moynihan, and Tony O'Keeffe tracing the Monsignor's maternal roots in North Cork. My regular intrusions into his household were invariably met with the greatest of hospitality both by himself and his wife Kay. In addition, I am grateful to his sister, Mrs Pearl Dineen, for making available to me the family photograph of the Monsignor with his parents and siblings. When I first met Hugh and Kay O'Flaherty in February in 2007 I became aware that their daughter Catherine was commencing work on a documentary outlining the Monsignor's wartime activities. She and I have co-operated fully since then, sharing information as it became available and I hope that between us we have ensured that the wonderful role the Monsignor played during the Second World War becomes known to a wider audience.

It has been my privilege for over twenty years now to have worked as a member of a highly competent and dedicated team of people. Even in such stellar company one comes across truly outstanding people from time to time. Happily for me, the two with whom I work most closely on a daily basis, Pauline Duffy and Róisín Harpur, most definitely fall into that category. They have given generously of their professional expertise in helping me with this project. For this and for so much else, I am eternally in their debt.

Finally, I wish to express my sincere thanks to Mary, Ciara and particularly Aoife for their practical assistance and support, which made it possible for me to realise my ambition to tell Hugh O'Flaherty's story.

Brian Fleming
Dublin
January 2008

Cast of Characters

The Rome Escape Organisation
Monsignor Hugh O'Flaherty, the founder of the organisation.
John May, a member of the Council of Three.
Count Sarsfield Salazar, a member of the Council of Three.
Major Sam Derry, the senior British officer involved in the organisation from late November 1943.

The Helpers
The Irish: Delia Murphy, Blon Kiernan, Frs Buckley, Claffey, Treacy, Lenan, Madden, Roche, Twomey, Forsythe and Brother Humilis.
The Maltese: Mrs Henrietta Chevalier, Brother Pace, Frs Galea, Borg and Gatt.
The British: Lts Simpson and Furman, Molly Stanley, Hugh Montgomery, Flt. Lt. Garrad-Cole and Major D'Arcy Mander.
The New Zealanders: Frs Sneddon and Flanagan.
The Czechoslovak: Private Joe Pollak.
The American: Monsignor Joseph McGeogh.
The Yugoslavs: Milko Scofic and Lt. Ristic Cedomir.
The Dutch: Fr Anselmo Musters.
The French: Jean de Blesson and François de Vial.
The Greeks: Evangelo Averoff and Theodoro Meletiou.
The Russian: Fr Borotheo Bezchctnoff.
The Italians: Renzo and Adrienne Lucidi, Princess Nini Pallavicini, Fr Giuseppe Clozner, Secundo Constantini, Giuseppe Gonzi, Sandro Cottich, Mimo Trapani, Fernando Giustini, Giovanni Cecarelli, the Pestalozza family, Prince Filippo Doria Pamphilj, Iride and Maria Imperoli, Prince Caracciolo and scores of others whose courageous support for the work of the organisation was crucial.

The Diplomats

Dr Thomas Kiernan, Irish Minister to the Holy See.
Michael MacWhite, Irish Minister to Italy.
Sir D'Arcy Osborne, British Minister to the Holy See.
Harold H. Tittmann, United States Chargé d'Affaires to the Holy See.
Ernst von Weizsaecker, German Ambassador to the Holy See.

The Vatican

Pope Pius XII, (Eugenio Pacelli, a native of Rome).
Cardinal Luigi Maglione, Secretary of State.
Monsignor Giovanni Battista Montini, Under Secretary for Ordinary Affairs (subsequently Pope Paul VI).
Monsignor Domenico Tardini, Under Secretary for Extraordinary Affairs.

The Allies

General Harold Alexander, Supreme Allied Commander.
Lieutenant General Mark W. Clark, senior American officer.

The Nazis/Fascists

Lieutenant Colonel Herbert Kappler, Head of the Gestapo in Rome.
Pietro Caruso, Fascist Chief of Police.
Pietro Koch, Chief of the Fascist Political Police Squad.
Field Marshal Albert Kesselring, Supreme German Army Commander in Italy.

The Observers

Mother Mary St Luke, an American nun living in Rome who published her diaries under the pseudonym, Jane Scrivener. Excerpts from her diary are referenced and dated in the text, for the convenience of the reader, as well as in the more conventional manner.

Michael MacWhite, an Irish diplomat living in Rome. Excerpts from his archive – including letters to the Department of Foreign Affairs, coded cablegrams and diary entries – are referenced and dated in the text, for the convenience of the reader, as well as in the more conventional manner.

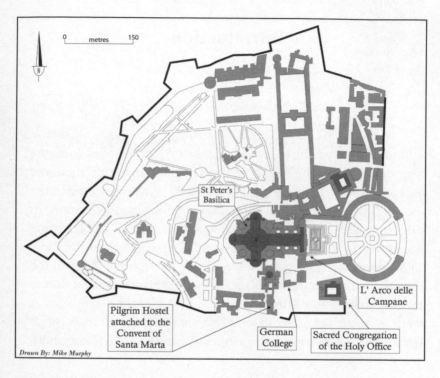

St Peter's
Basilica

L' Arco delle
Campane

Pilgrim Hostel
attached to the
Convent of
Santa Marta

German
College

Sacred Congregation
of the Holy Office

Drawn By: Mike Murphy

Map of the Vatican

Introduction

On Monday 10 June 1940, the dictator Benito Mussolini announced to the Italian people that their country would enter the War on the following day as partners of Germany. Until then, the career of Monsignor Hugh O'Flaherty, a Kerryman working in the Vatican, had been relatively routine. Following ordination in 1925, he fulfilled various roles in the Church, before being appointed to a position at the Sacred Congregation of the Holy Office in 1936. However, his speedy rise through the ranks of the Vatican civil service is a clear indication that he was a man of some considerable ability. The events of the War years illustrate that, as well as being an able man, O'Flaherty possessed truly great qualities of leadership, ingenuity, compassion and courage, both physical and moral.

Early on in the War, O'Flaherty was merely an observer. As he remarked to a friend later, 'When this War started I used to listen to broadcasts from both sides. All propaganda, of course, and both making the same terrible charges against the other. I frankly didn't know which side to believe – until they started rounding up the Jews in Rome. They treated them like beasts, making old men and respectable women get down on their knees and scrub the roads. You know the sort of thing that happened after that; it got worse and worse, and I knew then which side I had to believe.'

As he was well known in the city, many of those being hounded by the authorities began to seek his help. With assistance from many of his colleagues in religious life and local civilians, he began to hide and care for those on the run. Prominent among his

1

most active helpers were a number of Irish people. The Italians surrendered in the summer of 1943 and many Allied prisoners escaped as their warders left their posts. The numbers seeking help began to increase and by that autumn he had placed over a thousand people in safety in Rome and the surrounding areas. Some British officers, who were escapees themselves, moved in to help him and his friends at that stage.

The Nazis became aware of his activities and actively set about trying to capture him with the result that a deadly game of hide-and-seek began. If captured, he would certainly have been tortured and killed. However, he continued his work, often walking the streets of Rome in various disguises. It was for this sort of activity that he earned the nickname 'The Pimpernel of the Vatican'.

By the time of the Liberation of Rome in the summer of 1944, he and those whom he inspired had ensured the safety of more than 6,500 people, including 2,000 or so civilians.

For his outstanding contribution to the welfare of his fellow man, O'Flaherty was honoured by many governments, including the British (a CBE) and the Americans (a Medal of Freedom with Silver Palm). Yet, strangely, this truly remarkable man's story is not well known in his native Ireland. Sadly, no civil authority at any level has commemorated his extraordinary achievements. I hope that by writing this account the position will be rectified somewhat.

Brian Fleming

1

Rome 1941

The First World War was a bitter episode for the Italian people. Indeed the experiences which the Italians had during that war and its immediate aftermath explain, more or less completely, the course of Italian history for the next 25 years. From the time they joined the war until its end, the Italian armies were in battle on the Austrian front displaying great heroism without gaining a hugely significant amount of ground. However, tragically, they lost 600,000 of their men in a three-year period. Despite the fact that they were on the victorious side, Italy gained very little from the outcome of the war. France and Britain divided the main spoils between them and Italy's only significant gain was a small piece of what had formerly been Austria. In addition, in 1921 when the US and Britain agreed to fix treaty limits on the size of the fleet which the various Allied powers were to operate, Italy was forced to accept limitations which resulted in an entitlement to the same naval strength in the Mediterranean as the British Royal Navy. Clearly this was a direct insult to Italian national pride.

Throughout this period Italy was fairly unsettled. There was a clear disparity between what Italians felt they were entitled to after the war as members of the victorious Allied side, most particularly in light of the huge level of human sacrifice involved for them, and what had been assigned to them. Veterans and their families and others, mainly in the working and lower middle classes, were deeply dissatisfied with this situation. In addition, it was a time of recession and unemployment and the rise of extreme nationalism. Strikes and rumours of revolution were the order of the day. These unsettled conditions proved to be an ideal breeding ground for the rise of Fascism. In 1922 the King, Victor Emmanuel III, invited Benito Mussolini, leader of the Fascist group, to form a government. Within four years, Mussolini had effectively become a dictator, outlawing all other political parties, undermining civil liberties and imposing a totalitarian regime. At the same time, he managed to gain popularity by propaganda, public works projects, and, most particularly, by creating the appearance of order.

In 1929 the Lateran Treaty was concluded between Mussolini's Government and the Papacy. In the eyes of the Italian people this gave Mussolini further status. Under the terms of the Lateran Treaty, that part of Rome which comprises the Vatican and St Peter's became an independent sovereign state governed by the Pope. In addition, the Treaty allowed for papal governance of extra-territorial properties belonging to the Catholic Church in various parts of the city, including the Basilicas of St John Lateran, St Paul and St Maria Maggiore, together with all the buildings connected with them. Other properties included the offices of the Propagation of the Faith and of the Holy Office near St Peter's and the papal residence at Castelgandolfo. This essentially gave these buildings the same status as a foreign embassy has nowadays. The entire extent of the Vatican City itself is 108 acres and it is wholly contained in Rome, making it the smallest state in the world. The usual population based in the Vatican is approximately 500. Besides Pope Pius XII, the other senior officials in the Vatican when the Second World War started were Cardinal Maglione, Secretary of State, and his two assistants, Monsignor Montini, Under Secretary for Ordinary Affairs (essentially internal Vatican/Church matters) and Monsignor Tardini, Under Secretary for Extraordinary Affairs (essentially external issues). Monsignor Montini afterwards became Pope Paul VI.

Given the origins of the movement, it is not surprising that the Fascist Government adopted an expansionist foreign policy based on aggression. As early as 1919, at the foundation of the Fascist Movement, Mussolini was articulating the case that Italy needed more territory for her growing population. In 1935–6 the Italian army invaded and conquered Ethiopia and also in 1936 Italy sent troops to support Franco in the Spanish Civil War. Later that year Mussolini and Hitler established the Rome–Berlin Axis. In 1939 Italy took over Albania, and the two dictators, Hitler and Mussolini, concluded a military alliance known as the Pact of Steel. This agreement was signed on 22 May causing great concern to those within the Vatican who viewed any close relationship between Italy and Hitler as dangerous.

The war between Britain and France on the one hand, and Germany on the other, began on 3 September 1939. Serious efforts which were already under way in the US and Great Britain to keep Italy out of any war were immediately accelerated. The then American President, Roosevelt, was already acquainted with the Pope. Pope Pius XII, when he was a Cardinal, had visited the US in November 1936. At that stage there were no formal diplomatic links between the US and the Holy See, but Roosevelt sent the Ambassador in London, Joseph Kennedy, as a Special Envoy of the President to the Coronation Ceremony when the then Cardinal Pacelli became Pope in March 1939. This was the first time an American President had been represented at such an occasion. (As it happens, a future American President was there also, as John Fitzgerald Kennedy attended with his father.) President Roosevelt had concluded that, in the event of war, establishing some sort of working relationship with the Holy See might prove useful. The Vatican at that time had representatives in a total of 72 countries throughout the world from which it could gather significant information. In addition, 38 countries had official representation at the Holy See. The President decided to go ahead with establishing this link but it left him with a political problem. If he decided to send an official representative in the normal way, it would require a vote in the Houses of Congress to provide the necessary funds. It was doubtful that he would be successful in this because there was a strong feeling then current in the US of the need to separate church and state. In public relations terms, while the decision of the President would be popular with Catholic voters, it would alienate Protestants. As a way around this problem he decided to send a personal representative of himself as distinct from an envoy of the US Government. To obviate the need for funding, which could be provided only by a favourable vote in Congress, he needed to find a man who would require no payment. The President identified Myron Taylor as just such a man. At that stage, Taylor was President of the United States Steel Corporation. He was an Episcopalian and had a keen interest in the role of churches and churchmen in contributing to the moral order. He also had a knowledge of, and interest in, Italy and already owned property near Florence.

In his Christmas 1939 message to the Pope, the President announced the appointment of Taylor. It resulted in some criticism domestically but not of a hugely significant nature. Officially Taylor's appointment was to address refugee issues which were expected to arise particularly from the situation of Jews living in Germany and German-occupied territory. He had previously served on the President's Inter-Governmental Committee on Political Refugees in 1938 and so had a track record in that regard. As he agreed to serve without a salary, and his expenses were paid from funds allocated to the Committee on Refugees, the President did not need the approval of the Houses of Congress for his appointment.

Taylor arrived in Rome in early 1940 and immediately linked up with the British Minister to the Holy See, D'Arcy Osborne, and the French Ambassador, Charles-Roux. The US State Department was directed by the President to supply logistical support to Taylor and this took the form of Harold Tittmann who was then Consul General in Geneva. The diplomats, working with the Pope and the Vatican authorities, engaged in extensive efforts over the next few months to keep Italy out of the War. For example, Taylor had seven different appointments with the Pope in the period from 27 May to 23 June which was an unprecedented number of meetings over such a short period for a foreign diplomat. The general view was that President Roosevelt was far more likely to have an influence on Mussolini than anyone else. Indeed, even as early as the first week of 1940, the President was proposing to the Italian Government a common approach by Mussolini, the Pope and himself to restore peace in Europe. Furthermore, he indicated the desire for a conference with the Italian leader some time during the course of the year. Subsequently he sent the Under Secretary of State, Sumner Welles, on a visit to Rome during which he met Mussolini and emphasised again the President's anxiety that Italy would enter the War. In the meantime, the British Government was making clear to the Italian authorities that they had friendly relations with many governments, some of which were governed in a similar manner to Italy and that they would draw clear distinctions between the Nazis of Hitler and the Fascists of Mussolini. On 19 April Taylor telegraphed Roosevelt advising that he had conferred with the Cardinal Secretary of State in the Vatican, Maglione, and the representatives of various European countries at the Holy See, and all were agreed that the situation in relation to Italian neutrality was now approaching a critical juncture. They recommended that the President and the Pope engage in parallel appeals to Mussolini to keep out of the War. This suggestion, after some delay, was put into effect.

During all this time the Italian Foreign Minister was Count Ciano. He was Mussolini's son-in-law, being married to the Dictator's favourite daughter, Edda. Ciano had signed the Axis agreement with Germany on behalf of Italy but soon began to doubt the value of the link. He was one of those active in trying to persuade Mussolini not to join the War. Under the original Axis Agreement the Italian understanding was that war, if it were to happen, would not commence before 1943. Although he shared the Duce's expansionist policies, Ciano was acutely aware that Italy was in no position to engage in a prolonged war effort. He was also sensitive to the fact that among the public there was little enthusiasm for such a policy. Unfortunately, his advice, as well as the diplomatic efforts being made by the Vatican and various foreign governments, fell on deaf ears. Allied diplomats and Vatican authorities who were working to keep Italy out of the War did not foresee the quick collapse of France and the British withdrawal from Dunkirk in late May. Mussolini was, most likely, influenced by the fact that France had fallen and he thought at that point that he was joining the winning side. On Monday 10 June he announced to the Italian people that they would be at war the following day as partners of Germany.

The partnership between Germany and Italy was never one of equals. Italy's economy could only support a fraction of the military expenditure of Germany. The Italian armed forces had been allowed to decline in numbers since the previous war and emigration to the US had increased greatly. Much of the equipment which the Italian armed forces had was seriously outdated.

In relation to Italy's participation in the War, there was also a question mark as to public opinion. The Italians traditionally had little or no enmity towards the various Allied countries. For a long time, there had been close connections between the Italian and English upper classes and there was a high level of Anglophilia among the various noble families in Rome. The Italian working class had a high regard for the US. Many of their counterparts, including family members, had emigrated to America and they were strongly aware of the negative views of Nazism held in that country.

Italy's entry into the War immediately raised questions for the diplomats who were living in Rome representing those countries with whom Italy was now at war. The Lateran Treaty had clauses to govern just such a situation but they were somewhat vague. The Vatican Secretary of State, Cardinal Maglione, had raised this issue with the authorities as early as 1938. There were differing opinions held within the Italian Government – between the authorities in Foreign Affairs, the War Office and the Ministry of the Interior – so no clear response was issued. Eventually in May 1940 the Italian Government informed the Holy See that the diplomats from countries who might eventually be at war with Italy would have to leave and take up residence in a neutral country or move into the Vatican. At the invitation of the Pope, D'Arcy Osborne moved into the Vatican, as did the French and Polish Ambassadors among others, the week after Italy declared war. They were located in a pilgrim hostel attached to the Convent of Santa Marta on the south side of St Peter's Square. As the French had appointed a new Ambassador, d'Ormesson, the British Minister D'Arcy Osborne was now the senior diplomat among this group. In the early days, the facilities in the accommodation were fairly limited and D'Arcy Osborne found himself having to use Monsignor Montini's apartments for taking a bath. The two men got to know each other and became close friends during the succeeding months and years.

Of course the Italian authorities laid down some conditions. The diplomats representing those countries were now enemies of Italy, and so had to reside within the Vatican and not cross the border into Italy. For exceptional reasons, however, they were allowed to ask for permission to leave the Vatican and go into Rome. If this were granted, they were to be continuously escorted by a police officer. They were not allowed to send any telegrams in code. They were allowed make official communications to their governments but only in respect of their work as envoys to the Holy See. This excluded any reference to matters in relation to Italy. Their families were allowed to go to the seaside during hot weather, visiting the resort at Fregene. The diplomatic cars could leave the Vatican and go straight out to Fregene without going through the city centre and so avoid any embarrassment to the Italian Government.

By contrast the Irish representatives were there on behalf of a neutral country and so did not have to move into the Vatican. The Irish Minister at that time was Dr T. J. Kiernan. Thomas Kiernan was born in 1897 in Dublin and educated at St Mary's College, Rathmines and University College Dublin. He joined the Civil Service in the offices of the Inspector of Taxes in 1916 and was stationed in Galway from 1922 onwards. There he met his future wife, Delia Murphy. They became engaged a couple of years later. Both sets of parents disapproved of the engagement. It is easy to understand why the parents were concerned that this might not be an ideal match as the two had completely different personalities. Kiernan at that stage had already taken his Master's and intended doing a Ph.D. with a view possibly to taking up an academic career. Delia Murphy on the other hand had no interest in such a career and was very much into the social life of Galway. She was, even at that young age, a noted singer. Despite the disapproval of their parents, they got married in February 1924 at University Church in Dublin. Sadly, neither set of parents attended. In April 1924 Kiernan took up an appointment in London as Secretary to Commissioner McNeill in the High Commission Office. He completed his Doctorate at London University.

It is fair to say they were an odd couple. A friend at that time, the distinguished civil servant and author León Ó Broin, noted the contrast:

> I found him gentlemanly, courteous and desperately discreet. He was a retiring quiet man who smoked incessantly and I would say highly strung. He was very good looking, almost effeminate; and she was handsome, too, but bustling, almost rough. I wondered how they fitted into the Embassy scene abroad.[1]

Another friend, the actor, Liam Redmond, observes:

> Delia was an extrovert, she liked people who had the same openness as herself, and they liked her. Women with social pretensions and prissy men did not care for her. She just thought such people ridiculous and, typically she would seek out someone who was less hidebound by convention with whom she could have a bit of 'craic'. If possible at all, she would start a sing-song and soon she would have everyone around her singing along in the chorus.[2]

However their different strengths were to prove useful in the diplomatic service. She was a very well organised and generous hostess whereas her husband was not at all keen on entertaining. As her future son-in-law remarked some years later:

> She was well able for the entertaining side of diplomatic life and I could imagine her taking on anything. I could imagine, however, stuffy formal occasions being very trying for her, but then she could get a laugh out of those. She was totally unaware of any social or class distinction.[3]

As the years passed, Kiernan's career took a few interesting turns. The move to London had meant a transfer from Finance to Foreign Affairs and then in the mid 1930s he was transferred again to the Department of Post and Telegraphs on taking up an appointment as Director of Programmes at Radio Éireann. In the meantime, his wife was becoming increasingly well known as a singer and she had begun to record songs which were released by HMV later in that decade. She was encouraged in developing her musical career by Count John McCormack and the famous soprano, Margaret Burke Sheridan, and undoubtedly her husband's role as Director of Programmes was of assistance. Kiernan was a man of great integrity so it is unlikely that he ever asked anyone to play her music. At the same time, the fact that he was Director is likely to have influenced the selection of music in Radio Éireann. At one of the concerts she gave during those years we see an early example of her courage. She was singing at a concert in the Ulster Hall, Belfast, in April 1941 when the German bombers arrived. The *Irish News* reports:

> The raid revealed many heroes and heroines among quite ordinary people in the city. The bravery of Delia Murphy, wife of Dr Kiernan, Director of Radio Éireann, Dublin, during the height of the blitz, has been the subject of much discussion in Belfast. She was singing at a céilidhe in a large city hall. As bombs rained down, many of the women present became fearful of the consequences. Miss Murphy, however, remained perfectly cool, and kept singing continuously, asking those present to join her.[4]

Shortly after that, there was another significant change in her husband's career when he was appointed as a member of the Diplomatic Service in October 1941 to what was seen to be a very important post: Minister Plenipotentiary to the Holy See.

The Irish Government policy throughout the War was to remain neutral. Throughout this period the Taoiseach (Prime Minister), Éamon de Valera, also occupied the position of Minister for External Affairs (now Foreign Affairs). His chief adviser was Joseph Walshe, Secretary of the Department of External Affairs. In the early stages of the War, Walshe was of the view that Germany would almost certainly win:

> Britain's defeat has been placed beyond all doubt. France has capitulated. The entire coastline of Europe from the Arctic to the Pyrenees is in the hands of the strongest power in the world which can call upon the industrial resources of all Europe and Asia in an unbroken geographical continuity as far as the Pacific Ocean. Neither time nor gold can beat Germany.[5]
>
> (July 1940)

So, while at an unofficial level Walshe was willing to co-operate with the British, he saw it as prudent from the Irish point of view to stay neutral. This view coincided with the Taoiseach's. Aside from any political considerations, the country was in no position to engage in any serious level of conflict. The army had 7,600 members and suffered from a serious shortage of equipment. The Navy had two vessels and three motor torpedo boats. The Air Corps was similarly equipped. At the beginning and during the early years of the War, Walshe maintained his pessimistic view of the situation.

However, as the War progressed, there is no doubt that assistance was given to the Allied side at an informal level, including the sharing of intelligence and the granting of permission for Allied aircraft to fly over Irish territory in north Donegal to give them more direct access to the Atlantic. As time went by, the Irish authorities distinguished between operational and non-operational flights. By implementing this policy they ensured that most British and American planes which landed on Irish soil were allowed to leave as these were interpreted as being non-operational flights. By contrast, it was highly unlikely that any German plane would make a flight across Irish soil that would qualify as non-operational. These policies, however, were governed by strict censorship arrangements which were then in operation in the country and so were not generally known. As regards activities abroad, the Government was very anxious that the policy of strict neutrality would be observed. Instructions were sent out to staff working in the diplomatic service to ensure that this policy of neutrality was implemented.

> The Taoiseach wishes to remind all our staffs abroad, and this also applies to wives, that imprudent and un-neutral expressions of views reach places for which they are not intended and might have serious repercussions on the results of the policy of neutrality which the Government has pursued as the only means of preserving the independence of the nation and the lives of the people . . . The Taoiseach requires from all the strictest adherence to the foregoing instruction.[6]
> (14 June 1941)

By then, the Government had secured an undertaking from the German Minister that his country's intention was not to violate Ireland's neutrality and above all not to invade Ireland. Minister Kiernan was careful to implement the Taoiseach's instruction to the letter. For example, in one of his reports back to the authorities in Dublin (27 March 1943), he comments:

> I have met, socially, the Diplomats of the Axis and Allied Countries in about equal measure and have been careful to avoid giving any impression of stressing social acquaintance in any direction.[7]

The other senior Irish diplomat in Rome was Michael MacWhite, who was Minister at the Irish Embassy to the Italian Government. Michael MacWhite was born at Reenogreena near Glandore in West Cork on 8 May 1883. His father died in 1900 when Michael was seventeen. At that stage he came to Dublin to sit an examination for the British Civil Service and, during his visit to the city, met Arthur Griffith. They became lifelong friends. MacWhite was successful in the examination and moved to London to take up a position. At the age of eighteen he was Secretary of the Irish National Club in London and very well regarded in Irish circles there. He left London in the early years of the last century and did some travelling. He fought for Bulgaria in the first Balkan War in 1912, then joined the French Foreign Legion in 1913 and subsequently saw action in France, Greece and Turkey. He was wounded at Gallipoli and Macedonia and received the *Croix de Guerre* three times for his courage in battle. Following the war, he returned to Dublin and contacted his old friend Arthur Griffith with an offer to assist in the setting up of the new State. As a result, he became one of the founders of the Department of Foreign Affairs and saw service in various countries including the US. He was appointed to Rome in 1938. Clearly Arthur Griffith held Michael MacWhite in high esteem and indeed the evidence suggests he had plans to encourage the Corkman to become involved in active politics with a view to filling the role of Minister for External Affairs. Unfortunately, the premature death of Griffith in 1922 meant that these ideas never came to fruition.

2

A Young Priest in The Vatican

Hugh O'Flaherty was born in February 1898. His father, James O'Flaherty, was from the Headford area of Galway and joined the Royal Irish Constabulary (RIC) in 1881 at the age of about nineteen. (He is listed as 'Flaherty' in the records.) Having served for short periods in Longford and Mayo he moved to take up duty in Cork in 1885 where he served until 1897. During the latter years of his placement there he was assigned to the barracks at Glashykinlen. While there he met Margaret Murphy whose family farmed at Lisrobin, Kiskeam near Boherbue in County Cork. They got married in June 1897 and the following month they moved to live in Kerry as he had been transferred to a new posting in Tralee where he served for a number of years before being transferred subsequently to Killarney.

The tradition in the Murphy family, as indeed in many others at that time, was for the expectant mother to return to her maternal home so that her own mother could assist with the birth, particularly in the case of the first born. Accordingly, Hugh O'Flaherty was born in Cork. However, he would insist for the rest of his life that he was a Kerryman through and through (although he adopted a neutral position between Cork and Kerry, at least for a few minutes, when on one occasion he was honoured with the invitation to throw in the ball at a Munster Final).

James O'Flaherty resigned from the RIC in 1909 to take up the position of caretaker and caddy-master at the Killarney Golf Club which was then located at Deerpark on lands donated by Lord Kenmare, the major landlord in the area. The O'Flaherty family lived in the front lodge on the property, so essentially they had access to the golf course every day. This is where Hugh's lifelong love affair with the sport of golf commenced. He turned out to be fairly expert at the game, managing to get his handicap down to low single figures, close to scratch.

In 1913 Hugh found himself involved as a witness in a court case. Three women came to hold a meeting in Killarney as part of the suffragette movement. They applied for permission to use the Town Hall but were told it was not available. They got a similar response from Lord Kenmare when they applied for permission to use the Golf Clubhouse, so they ended up holding their campaign meeting in the open air. The day after the meeting, the Golf Clubhouse burned down. James O'Flaherty gave evidence that he went to bed shortly after 11.00 p.m. and when he woke at 5.00 a.m. the clubhouse was burning. Hugh gave evidence that the Club Secretary left at 6.30 p.m. the previous evening and there was no sign of any fire. He also said that he found a suffragette emblem on the premises. The club was awarded damages more or less to the full amount they sought in court.

At the age of fifteen Hugh secured a Junior Teaching Assistant post in the Presentation Brothers School there. Subsequently, he won a scholarship to teacher training but failed his Diploma examinations, most likely due to a bout of illness which interfered with his studies towards the end. However, during all of this time his ambition was to join the priesthood. He was concerned that the pursuit of this vocation would place additional financial hardship on the family and was nervous of approaching his father on the matter. He decided that the best course of action was to enlist the assistance of his only sister, Bride, who, it would seem, was 'the apple of her father's eye'. He need not have worried. When Bride approached her father, his response was, 'I would sell the house to make a priest of him.'

He successfully applied to Mungret College in Limerick which was an institution run by the Jesuit Order preparing young boys for the priesthood on the missions. He joined Mungret in 1918. While he made excellent progress in his studies, he was more noted for his prowess in the sports area: golf, handball, hurling, boxing and swimming were among his favourite pastimes.

This was a difficult period in Irish history and the young students in Mungret were well aware of the various atrocities being committed by the occupying British forces at that time. Indeed, O'Flaherty's father resigned from the RIC, like many of his colleagues, rather than find himself in confrontational situations with neighbours while fulfilling his duties. Hugh himself had a brush with the law in 1921. He and two of his colleagues had walked from Mungret into Limerick to pay their respects at the houses of two prominent citizens who had been shot the previous night. On their way home, all three were arrested and held, until released at the request of the Rector of Mungret College who had been tipped off that his students were in difficulty.

Later in 1921, O'Flaherty was sponsored by the religious authorities in Cape Town, South Africa, and sent to Rome to continue his studies. He was assigned to the Propaganda College whose objective was to prepare young men for work in the missions. During his time there he distinguished himself academically and he qualified in 1925. He was ordained by Cardinal van Rossum on 20 December 1925 and celebrated his first Mass the following day.

His correspondence home to a range of family members during these years highlights the characteristics and values which he brought to bear on his subsequent work. Particularly noteworthy are his humility, a gentle nature, care and concern for others (most particularly his parents), the strength of his vocation, a sense of humour and a willingness to help anyone – whether relative, friend or distant acquaintance – who might be visiting Rome. In addition of course he kept his family up to date on his developing career and was always anxious to hear news of home. For example, he wrote to his sister in July 1925 regarding his success in the examination for the Licentiate in Theology (L.S.T.):

> I just 'flucked' [fluked] through and no more – the narrowest shave I ever had . . . I was fortunate to slip through . . . I went in for the exam in the evening . . . with a cold perspiration all over because five went in that morning and only one got through the ordeal with success! Even the two Irishmen

before me fell and here was I the sole hope of old Ireland and
Mungret going in to try and lift the flag from the dust. Four
professors were before me but only three can examine. For
the first two I did splendid thanks to the prayers of many
friends and St Theresa. But the third went well for half time
and he glued me to the chair with rockers and the others
helped him to crush and reduce the points which were mine
in the beginning . . . However, they gave me the Degree and
I have it.[1]

He contrasts his success in the Degree examination and the
consequent entitlement he now had to place three letters after his
name with the importance of his vocation:

But there are also three letters before Hugh! 'Rev' after July
12th. It was a great day and as usual when I am happy and the
Lord showers blessings on me, then instead of laughing and
thanking Him I cry, which of course is mother's weakness.[2]

He then advises his sister that he was thinking of going on for a
Doctorate in Theology.

Though it seems an impossible thing . . . Father H. J. is nicer
than Doctor H. J. so what was I to do. The Rector decided the
question without knowing it. I was taken from my own
fellows and made Prefect of twenty-seven of the liveliest wires
in the house and so busy that I have not seen any of the
papers Chris sent.[3]

The Rector he refers to is Monsignor Torquato Dini who was to
prove a very valuable friend and mentor to the young Irishman
over the next decade or so. He had obviously seen great potential
in O'Flaherty and, as we can see from the letter, promoted him to
work in the College as soon as he qualified and encouraged him to
complete his further studies. During the next few years, O'Flaherty
secured three Doctorates – in Divinity, Philosophy and Canon Law
– and was promoted to the rank of Monsignor. Such a promotion
so early in his career (he was, after all, still in his early thirties)
underlines the high regard in which he was held in the Vatican.

Of course the Bishop in Cape Town, Dr O'Reilly, was anxious

to secure the services of the priest his diocese had sponsored. In December of 1926 O'Flaherty reports back to his parents:

> The Rector told me he had a great struggle with the Bishop and who would blame the poor man; he has only thirty-three priests for such a big place.[4]

The following year he wrote directly to the Bishop confirming that he was available:

> Last June I was ready to leave and had my work rushed in order to prepare for my journey to the Cape but the Cardinal Prefect told me I was to stay longer and he intended to write and let you know. Monsignor Dini also told me it was necessary to stay a little longer and when I said you needed priests he replied that he would compensate my loss by giving you a place for another student next year.[5]

This sort of negotiation went on for a number of years. Monsignor Dini was in the strategic position of being able to assign places in the College for young students to various dioceses across the world. O'Flaherty reported back to his mother in May 1928 that although places were scarce the Bishop of Cape Town had met with some success.

> Now he had got four free places and I shall very soon tell him that he would not have one only for Monsignor Dini and yours truly. But he will not be content. Give a man a flowerbed and he will want your backyard.[6]

As we have seen, living in Italy at that time was very interesting from a political point of view. O'Flaherty wrote back to his sister in June 1927 prompting her to tell her husband Chris Sheehan, who was a shopkeeper, about the latest regulations governing the retail trade and other matters in Rome.

> How is Chris? Give him my very best wishes. He would laugh if he was in Italy at present. They are making all kinds of laws. Yesterday there was published a list of shopkeepers who were selling inferior goods and who were defrauding the public. They must now close. Besides the latest law makes

people walk in the right hand side . . . added to this we have the unmarried tax and a tax for those married people who have no children. Il Duce is doing well.[7]

The Monsignor had a lifelong interest in the latest gadgetry and by the summer of 1927 had secured the use of a typewriter and was also purchasing a machine from America for showing moving pictures. In a letter to his mother he reports:

I get a number of letters but have very little time to answer them and besides I hate writing letters for when I have written the letters for the College I am tired and cannot face my own. For the future I will answer my letters only every Sunday so that will save time during the week. However, I must not complain for the typewriter is handy and I can run off a letter in less than five minutes. Please do not say that if that is all the time it takes that you would expect one oftener for yours require more time.[8]

It is clear that he played golf at every opportunity though it was an expensive game in the Italy of that time.

It is a fine game but my pocket cannot play it so I must write on my clubs 'taboo'. Some time ago the Japanese Ambassador, before leaving for Japan, invited me to play with him and I was in good form. I astonished a good many there with the length of my drive; they all wondered why a priest should play so well for in this country they think a priest should live, eat, pray, sleep and die in the church and he is good for nothing else . . .The links are far from the City and besides to be a member one must know how to rob a bank and keep what is robbed.[9]

He also kept fit by playing handball and wrote home in July 1928 asking that his brother-in-law Chris would mail him two good handballs. 'Two is enough or otherwise I would have to pay a heavy tax.'[10]

Monsignor Dini and O'Flaherty looked after the wishes of the Bishop of Cape Town so well that the young Irishman continued to work in the Propaganda College for a number of years. However, a cloud appeared on the horizon in 1933. He wrote to his sister Bride in November of that year:

> I had a word privately that Monsignor Dini is going to Palestine as Apostolic Delegate; he will be made an Archbishop and will go there some time after Christmas; what is going to happen to your beloved brother is not yet known.[11]

He need not have worried; his mentor was looking after his interests and a couple of weeks later he was advised that he would be going to Palestine as Secretary to the Apostolic Delegate.

It is not surprising that Dini took Monsignor O'Flaherty with him as his Secretary, having earlier identified him as a young man of significant promise. Not long into the mission, however, Dini died suddenly and O'Flaherty had to step into the breach temporarily as Chargé d'Affaires. He carried out his duties to great effect and as a result was appointed, in 1934, as Secretary to the Apostolic Delegate to the Republics of Haiti and San Domingo. O'Flaherty spent just a year in this position. However, he was obviously successful in this role because, on his departure, he was decorated by the Presidents of each of the Republics for his work in relation to famine relief and helping to settle a border dispute. In 1936, he was called back to Rome and then sent to Czechoslovakia. He spent two years there before being summoned again to Rome and given a new appointment in the Sacred Congregation of the Holy Office.

O'Flaherty spent the next quarter of a century working in that Office. It was never made clear what his role had been in Czechoslovakia nor indeed did he talk about it himself. Obviously, it had been a fairly sensitive mission and the fact that it was assigned to him is a clear indication of the high regard in which he was held by his superiors. When he joined it, the Head of the Holy Office was Monsignor Alfredo Ottaviani who was then in the early stages of a distinguished career as a powerful force within the Vatican. These two men had completely different personalities: one outgoing, gregarious and ebullient, and the other austere, careful and extremely conservative. Notwithstanding this, a lifelong friendship developed between them, and there is no doubt that the support of Ottaviani was helpful to O'Flaherty in subsequent years when his unofficial activities came to the attention of the Church authorities.

During this time, O'Flaherty also began to develop a wide range of contacts among Roman society generally. Many of these he would have got to know when he became an active member of the Rome Golf Club. It seems there was a regulation at that time which prohibited priests in the Diocese of Rome from playing golf but this did not seem to bother either O'Flaherty or his immediate superior Ottaviani. Among the many people he got to know then were some members of the old Roman noble families who proved to be of great assistance to him later in his work. Vittoria, the Duchess of Sermoneta, recalls:

> I first met him at the Golf Club before the war, where he played a tip top game that I used to admire from a distance – it inspired awe in a rabbit like myself. At that time I did not know his name. When I heard in '41 that John Fox-Strangways, son of my dear friends the Ilchesters, was a prisoner-of-war and lying with a broken leg at a military hospital of Caserta, I wished to send him some books and a letter, and was told the best way would be to entrust the parcel to Monsignor O'Flaherty who lived in the Vatican. When he came to my house to fetch it I was surprised to discover he was the golfing priest I had so often seen. He then played golf no longer, for his time was fully engaged doing good service for all the unfortunates of any nationality that needed help . . .[12]

When the diplomats of the Allied powers moved into the Hospice of Santa Marta, O'Flaherty was living in the nearby German College. During most of his life in Rome, O'Flaherty lived in this College and he developed a lifelong admiration for the German people and made valiant efforts to conquer their language. Notwithstanding his expertise in Italian, French and Spanish, he always found the German language difficult.

The onset of the war inevitably created huge problems of refugees – homeless, displaced and missing persons – and the Holy

Office was assigned by the Pope the duty of dealing with all of those issues. This resulted in a new line of work for O'Flaherty. Within a year or so of Italy joining the War, there were tens of thousands of Allied prisoners of war in camps throughout the north of the country. The Pope asked the Papal Nuncio to Italy, Monsignor Bergoncini Duca, to visit these camps to check on the welfare of the prisoners. As Duca had no English, O'Flaherty was asked to go along with him to act as his secretary and interpreter.

They started the work at Easter 1941. The Nuncio took a fairly leisurely approach to this task, visiting one camp per day. However, O'Flaherty approached the role with his usual energy. He regularly hopped on a train and travelled back to Rome, at night-time, with up-to-date lists of names of those whom he had tracked down, to be broadcast promptly by Vatican radio. A New Zealander, Fr Owen Sneddon, worked there and was a friend of O'Flaherty's. While the scripts of his broadcast were prepared by the authorities, Sneddon regularly added in pieces of information which were of huge importance to next of kin at the request of the Irishman. Hugh would then make the train journey back and rejoin the Nuncio in time for the visit to the next camp the following morning. In this way, he could ensure that information would reach the next of kin as quickly as possible. He also cut through red tape to ensure that Red Cross parcels to prisoners were delivered as quickly as possible and he distributed thousands of books around the camps, including a prayer book that he compiled together with another Irish priest, Monsignor Thomas Ryan. O'Flaherty also campaigned successfully to have the number of doctors and Protestant chaplains in prisoner-of-war camps in the south of Italy increased to appropriate levels. His blithe disregard for regulations and red tape in carrying out these duties eventually caused problems. Pressure was brought to bear by the Fascist authorities in late 1942 and as a result he was asked by Vatican authorities to resign from his position with Monsignor Duca and he did so. However, before he left he lodged very effective complaints about the manner in which two Camp Commanders were treating the prisoners. As a result, these Commanders, at Modena and Piacenza, were relieved of their duties. We now know that in December 1942 the Italian censors had discovered a letter from a British prisoner of war to his home which said 'The Monsignor had told [them] that the war was going well.' Most likely this was the official reason given to the Vatican with the request that his appointment be terminated but:

> There is little doubt, however, that the real reason was the importunity with which Monsignor O'Flaherty championed the cause of all Allied Prisoners of War, persecuted Jews, anti-Fascists and refugees and thus disturbed the Italian Fascists' conscience and policy towards these unfortunate people.[13]

However, a couple of months later, he made an informal visit with a Monsignor Riberi to a prisoner-of-war camp for Australian and South African prisoners at Tuturano near Brindisi. After the visit, the local Fascist party reported to the authorities in Rome that the visit had raised the morale of the prisoners and lowered that of their guards.

Others had begun to notice him also. Michael MacWhite had been appointed in 1938 as the first Irish Envoy Extraordinary and Minister Plenipotentiary to the Italian Government. He had been one of the original members of the Department of External Affairs, along with Joseph Walshe, after independence. On 19 November 1942 he wrote to Walshe at the Department of External Affairs in Dublin:

> I have heard that Monsignor O'Flaherty came back from Ireland like a travelling postman . . . how he succeeded in obtaining a Vatican Passport for travelling to Ireland is a mystery to me as I doubt he had any official mission. Kiernan gave him a diplomatic visa. In view of his abuse of the privileges I don't think it advisable that he should get one again. After his return here, he was reprimanded by Montini for something or other and I gather the Questura has him now under observation. It will not surprise me if he finds himself in a concentration camp one of these days. A period there might develop in him a sense of proportion and responsibility.[14]

It is hard to understand the quite strong sentiments expressed in the report from the Irish Legation. It seems to imply that the

Monsignor's activities involved more than just cutting through red tape and bureaucratic difficulties when it suggests that the Questura (police headquarters) had him under observation. At the same time, the journey home to Ireland, presumably a fairly innocuous event, hardly seems to merit such strong condemnation. There is no evidence that there was any personal antagonism between the Monsignor and the diplomat. At the same time, MacWhite was a very acute and well-informed observer of the scene in Rome. Very little is known about O'Flaherty's unofficial activities on behalf of prisoners of war at this stage. MacWhite's report gives a strong reason to believe that the Monsignor had commenced this work as early as the autumn of 1942.

There seems to have been some tension between MacWhite and his counterpart at the Holy See, Kiernan. In December 1943, in a report back to the Department, Kiernan notes:

> MacWhite got very huffy with me and said I have no jurisdiction in Rome outside the strict Vatican territory and so on. But I do everything to avoid hurting his sensitivity. He wants me to report to him every time an Irish priest or religious comes to me about some 'protection' difficulty.[15]

Kiernan was not the sort of man who would hand over any of his responsibilities to another. However, MacWhite may have had reason to be careful in his dealings with Kiernan. As early as December 1942 a clear divergence emerges as to how things ought to be handled. MacWhite drafted a letter to Kiernan which he dated 10 December. As he did not sign it, it is reasonable to presume it was never sent. At the same time it is a clear reflection of his concerns:

> I have your letters of the 22nd and 23rd referring to certain action taken by you in connection with the protection of Irish property in Italy without first consulting me and note your preference for Departmental lessons in official correctness. You have, of course, your own way of doing things.
>
> Five weeks ago I had a cable from the Department instructing me to remain in Rome at all costs for the

protection of our citizens and in case I had to leave I was to ask the Holy See to arrange for their protection 'through Kiernan or otherwise'. Instead of arranging to have this done through the Nuncio, as I might have done in conformity with official correctness, I called you in for consultation and asked you to undertake it. This is my way of doing things.

When at your legation some weeks ago you were very insistent in urging me to fake a passport to permit a British prisoner of war to enter the Vatican, I suppose this is also a matter in regard to which you would prefer the Department to be the judge of your 'official correctness'.[16]

Early 1943 saw the turning point in the War, with the Russian success at Stalingrad and the Allied victory in North Africa. The Italian Fascist authorities began to tighten their grip on Rome as a result. As part of this exercise, they began a process of searching out leading figures in the city who they considered might be a focus of dissent in the months ahead. Notable among these were Jews and prominent Italian anti-Fascists who might provide leadership to the Romans. By this stage also, O'Flaherty's reputation as the person to approach if one needed assistance had become well established. Many people whose situation was now precarious had already got to know him at pre-war social events. As one of his closest colleagues described the situation some time later:

He has been at the Vatican since 1922, and seems to know everyone in Rome. Everybody knows Monsignor O'Flaherty – and, what is more important, they all adore him.[17]

Initially the Monsignor's role was merely to make suggestions to friends and acquaintances who felt that they might be in danger of arrest. He very quickly became a rallying point for those who were under threat, most particularly Jews and Anti-Fascists. He referred them to safe locations, usually monasteries or convents, where he felt they might find sanctuary. However, as fears grew and more and more raids became commonplace, his role developed a more active dimension. He began to hide some of those who approached him in his own place of residence which, ironically, was the

German College in Rome. This College had, over the years, been home to many German students and was under the care of a German Rector assisted by a staff of German-born nuns. In addition, it was home to a number of Vatican officials, including O'Flaherty. Although it was in the shadow of St Peter's, the College was not in the Vatican itself but had the status of an extra-territorial property. Quite soon it became home to some unofficial guests. One of the early arrivals was Princess Nini Pallavicini, a young widow and a member of one of the ancient noble Roman families. Many of these families were quite public in their opposition to the position of the Fascist Government on the War. The authorities were aware that an illegal radio was operating in a particular area of Rome and eventually traced it to Palazzo Rospigliosi-Pallavicini where the Princess lived. As a result, they launched a raid and Princess Nini narrowly escaped by jumping out a window. She immediately sought O'Flaherty's help. He moved her into the German College and, although a very substantial cash reward was posted for information leading to her arrest, she was never betrayed. She spent the rest of the War assisting him in his work, particularly in providing false identity documents for escapees. Regular supplies of such papers were issued to people who came to O'Flaherty for help. It has even been suggested that printing equipment belonging to the Vatican was used in this exercise.

Others whom he helped at that time were three soldiers from New Zealand who arrived at St Peter's seeking sanctuary. They had become acquainted with O'Flaherty on his visits to the prisoner-of-war camps and asked to meet him when they arrived in Rome. He immediately arranged sanctuary for all three within the Vatican.

More and more escapees were now heading towards Rome seeking assistance. While it is probably true to say that, by and large, they were safer in the countryside, Rome was a fairly obvious objective for anyone in those circumstances. The idea was to make contact with one's own embassy, or that of a neutral country, or indeed take advantage of the long-standing and worldwide tradition of sanctuary in monasteries, convents and other religious houses. Many of these people had escaped from the prisoner-of-war camps and others had managed to get away from their captors on train journeys which were bringing them to camps in Germany. In the early months, many of those who came to Rome managed to hide safely in the Vatican, which cannot have been too difficult given that it extends to approximately 10,000 rooms. We can be fairly certain that O'Flaherty was involved with many of these cases. However, the fact that such an escape route existed became well known. This embarrassed the Vatican authorities and compromised their diplomatic situation. Orders were issued to the Swiss Guard that anyone seeking refuge in the Vatican or on papal property was to be refused. This created a new difficulty for the Monsignor in his efforts to assist people. One of the first large groups he dealt with was fourteen British prisoners of war to whom the Swiss Guard had refused entry to the Vatican for sanctuary.

> Standing forlornly and dangerously conspicuous in the vast St Peter's Square, dressed in an assortment of clothes they had acquired somehow, they simply did not look like tourists or devout Catholics come to see the Pope. One of the Irish priests who live in St Monica's Monastery, opposite the Holy Office behind the Bernini Colonnade, approached them and soon found out their predicament. They were taken into St Monica's for an hour or two while O'Flaherty was consulted.[18]

O'Flaherty arranged with the help of a friend, Antonio Call, a policeman with strong anti-Fascist sympathies, to smuggle them into the Vatican two and three at a time. In light of the new arrangement, however, they were expelled the next day and so O'Flaherty with the help of Fr Giuseppe Clozner arranged to have them housed, rather incredibly, in an Italian police barracks where they were cared for by the staff until such time as the Germans occupied Rome the following September. Unfortunately, all but two were recaptured at that stage. However, this was an early indication of O'Flaherty's extensive range of contacts and the willingness of many people, irrespective of their circumstances, to help him.

Three South Africans, a Corporal De Villiers and two Privates, Crout and Dally, having escaped in the north of Italy, walked to Rome and sought O'Flaherty's help. He arranged to place them in private accommodation. En route there, he was stopped by three

German SS officers who fortunately only asked for directions. At the same time, he arranged for two American pilots, who had been forced to parachute near Rome, to be placed in safety. Then he heard that a Sergeant Wyndham was in hospital in Rome and, having arranged for his discharge, the Monsignor placed him with a family who were willing to help.

The Germans cast continuous doubts on the situation of the diplomats in the Vatican. In October 1942 after a visit by the Head of the Gestapo, Himmler, a story reached the Vatican that he had demanded the expulsion of all the diplomats, and it was only because the Italian authorities protested that a decision was made not to go ahead. Rumours ebbed and flowed for the remaining years of the War as to possible intrusions and takeovers of the Vatican by the German authorities. There were even suggestions from time to time of a plot to kidnap the Pope. It was also suggested that there were actually agents of the Gestapo in the Vatican. Information garnered by American code breakers, which was made public after the War, confirmed that this was in fact the case.

The legal situation in relation to the diplomats was not very clear. The wording of the Lateran Treaty was, as we have seen, fairly vague. Everyone knew that in these circumstances it was of huge importance that the Vatican and its diplomats behave in accordance with the conditions laid down for them. The reality for all of those living in the Vatican was indeed rather tenuous. The Vatican is an extremely small area and has no water supply of its own. At any stage, the Italians could have forced the situation by switching off the supply of this necessity.

In December 1941, the Japanese bombed Pearl Harbour and, in response, the Americans declared war. Taylor returned to Washington leaving Tittmann in charge of relations with the Holy See. In diplomatic terms, Tittmann's status was unclear. Essentially his role was to provide logistical support to a personal friend of the President of the United States, who had the status of Ambassador but not the rank or title. So while the Vatican authorities were happy to offer him the same sanctuary as D'Arcy Osborne and the others, the Italian Government was opposed. Roosevelt decided to face down any likely domestic opposition and, within a couple of days, Tittmann was appointed to the rank of Chargé d'Affaires. He took up residence in the Hospice Santa Marta on 16 November 1941 and quickly developed a close personal friendship with his British counterpart. This filled a gap for D'Arcy Osborne. Previously he had been very friendly with the French Ambassador, d'Ormesson. However, the latter had been withdrawn by the Vichy Government, which came to power after the collapse of France, and had been replaced by Bérard, who did not communicate with Allied diplomats at all.

The police and the Italian authorities had a good idea of the views of senior Vatican personnel on the political situation. Montini was regularly the focus of attack in the Fascist newspapers. The police relied for their information on Italian servants working in the Vatican, as well as undercover agents. They even went to the extent of stationing agents in churches to monitor those who might approach the clergy for help. D'Arcy Osborne was also a focus of attention as he was the leading Allied diplomat living within the Vatican. However, insofar as we know, the authorities had still not become aware of O'Flaherty and his activities to any significant degree. While the absence of records means that information is rather sketchy we can say with certainty now that by November 1943 O'Flaherty and his colleagues had placed in excess of a thousand people in safety.

3

The Germans Take Charge

The latter months of 1942 and early 1943 saw the beginnings of a re-evaluation of Italian involvement in the War by some in positions of authority. By March 1943, there were signs in army circles that many were willing to consider the possibility of a *coup d'état*. The British and American authorities began to consider the terms they would apply to any armistice should one be sought by the Italians. The possibility that the Pope might fulfil the role of peacemaker received active consideration inside and outside the Vatican. A message was transmitted to Mussolini by the Vatican authorities emphasising their concern at the damage that was being caused to Italy by the War and underlining that the Pope was available, as always, to do what he could to help alleviate the suffering of the people. Mussolini, however, still thought victory was possible and was not of a frame of mind to consider the possibility of surrender and so did not explore this offer of assistance. At the same time, suggestions came to him from the King and those around him that a change of policy would be appropriate. He informed the King that it would take three months to prepare for a possible peace move.

At the same time, he expected that there would be an attack in Sicily as the Allied Forces, following their victory in Tunisia, were now in a position to commit men to such a tactic. Hitler also anticipated such an attack and offered Mussolini five additional German divisions but this was declined. There is no doubt that Hitler was anxious to stiffen the resolve of Mussolini as he realised the strategic importance of the Italian Dictator to the German cause.

In Italy we can rely only on the Duce. There are strong fears that he may be got rid of or neutralised in some way. The Royal Family, all leading members of the Officer Corps, the clergy, the Jews and broad sectors of the Civil Society are hostile or negative towards us . . . the broad masses are apathetic and lacking in leadership.[1]

In the meantime, the British authorities were anxious to get D'Arcy Osborne home to be fully briefed on these moves, as communication on such delicate matters, other than in a face-to-face session, was highly dangerous. In accordance with the terms of the Lateran Treaty, Ambassadors to the Vatican had a free right of communication with their home country. However, Italy had made it a condition that this could only refer to matters within the Vatican. The papal authorities felt that they, as a result, had a moral obligation to come to the assistance of the diplomats who were facing difficulties in this regard and so offered the use of the Vatican diplomatic bag. These bags went by papal courier to Berne or Lisbon where they were handed over to the British Embassies and then in turn sent on to London. However, there was always the risk that information could be leaked and so the authorities in London were very anxious for a meeting. D'Arcy Osborne could only leave the Vatican with the permission of the Italian authorities. This he finally secured through the good offices of Monsignor Montini who used sympathetic contacts available to him in the Foreign Affairs section of the Italian Government. At that stage, some in authority were anxious for peace and so were willing to co-operate with the Vatican authorities whom they looked to as suitable mediators in these matters. D'Arcy Osborne left Rome on 18 April 1943 and returned on 8 June. On the day after his return he visited Monsignor Tardini and reported the official British Government line which was that Italy would have to surrender unconditionally. At the Casablanca Conference in January 1943, Roosevelt and Churchill had agreed that, in the event of Germany and or Japan seeking an armistice, the Allied position would be to require them to surrender unconditionally. There was no formal agreement with regard to Italy. The British Government was now taking the view that the same requirement for an unconditional surrender should apply, a position which D'Arcy Osborne felt was unduly harsh. No progress was made for the next few weeks. However, on 10 July the Allied Forces invaded Sicily. Although their progress was delayed, within four or five weeks they had taken the island. This experience made it clear to Italy's ruling class that they must change sides.

> The invasion of Sicily has, at last, obliged the mass of the Italian public to realise the seriousness of their military situation. Up to now they appeared indifferent and the enemy was so far away. Besides, the German Army was invincible. Today things have somewhat changed. The Allies have planted their feet solidly on Italian soil . . . Three weeks ago the Duce assured the Fascist leaders that any enemy soldier who polluted the sacred soil of Italy would not live to tell the tale. This was but a repetition of the cry from the other side of the Alps that the European fortress was unassailable.[2]
>
> (*MacWhite*, 15 July 1943)

Hitler had foreseen this and had flown to Italy to meet Mussolini, such was his level of concern. Mussolini, meanwhile, had promised the Italian King that at his meeting with Hitler he would raise the possibility of an Italian withdrawal from the War. When he did not fulfil this undertaking, the King decided that he must withdraw his support from the Dictator. At the same time, members of the Fascist Grand Council had requested Mussolini to call a meeting, which he did. This body had not met for a number of years and indeed had always been merely a rubber stamp, so the Dictator did not anticipate problems. However, at this meeting, which started on 24 July and ran into 25 July, a motion of no confidence in Mussolini was passed by nineteen votes to seven. Included among those speaking and voting in favour of this motion was his son-in-law, Count Ciano. Mussolini felt, however, that he still had the support of the King and would remain in power. He was due to have an audience with the King later that day but when he arrived, he was very quickly arrested. Marshal Badoglio was appointed Prime Minister by the King.

The most original creation of Fascism, said Mussolini one day, is the Grand Council. It expresses all the thoughts of the regime. It could even propose to modify the succession to the throne. Apparently, he did not anticipate that the time was not so far distant when the same Grand Council would appeal to the Monarchy to overthrow the man who had created it. And it was some of his erstwhile devoted supporters who took the initiative in the decision to do so . . . the sweeping nature of the defeat was apparently unexpected and would seem that Grandi who was indicated as the future duce had not even realised that the eclipse of Mussolini marked at the same time the collapse of the fascist regime and everything associated with it . . . The coup d'état had succeeded beyond the expectations of those who had plotted to bring it about. Without a hand being raised in his defence Mussolini was now behind prison bars reflecting perhaps on the instability of dictatorship. He had been ignominiously dismissed from office by a King whom he had humiliated and despised but who, nevertheless, waited patiently for the opportunity to resume his royal prerogatives . . . on the fateful Sunday morning of July 25th, Mussolini still had the destinies of Italy within his grasp . . . some hours later, as the long summer evening was drawing to a close, the Rome radio, to the general surprise, announced that the King had accepted the resignation of Mussolini and had invested Marshal Badoglio with full power. It did not take the Italian public very long to realise the full import of the laconic statement. The people rushed into the streets shouting with joy and crying out 'Long live the King', 'Long live free Italy' and 'Down with Mussolini'[3]

(*MacWhite*, 27 July 1943)

The Irish Legation was located quite close to Rome's central barracks and the railway station terminus. Thomas Kiernan felt that, in the light of the Allied bombing, this was a dangerous place to keep his family so they moved to live on a temporary basis in one of the Vatican's extra-territorial properties on the Via del Penitenziari close to St Peter's Basilica. He describes the outpouring of joy in Rome at the fall of Mussolini:

A few minutes before midnight we were raised from our beds by wild shouting of exultation. Broken-down cars loaded with young men were careering through Rome shouting their heads off. Mussolini is arrested . . . People who have been waiting like a condemned-to-death prisoner reacted now with all the wild abandon of reprieve. Not only reprieve, but complete liberty. Little did they, or any of us, anticipate that Rome's travail was only then about to begin . . . We dressed hurriedly and went out, following the stream of improvised traffic. Suddenly a flame lit up the darkness . . . Blocked in the chaos of traffic we saw the flames rise to light the great Basilica.[4]

The anti-Fascist forces within the city were breaking into the offices of the authorities and taking out furniture, paper, chairs and anything they could put their hands on and had lit a bonfire near St Peter's. Another observer, a Swiss journalist named de Wyss, was alert to the political significance of the comments of the people:

Hearing the news, people rushed into the streets just as they were; in night-gowns, night-shirts, pyjamas, some in trousers and bare to the waist, some in slippers, some barefoot, all howling, yelling, screaming . . . They shouted 'Abasso Mussolini' (down with Mussolini) . . . the publishing office of Il Tevere (a rabidly Fascist newspaper) was set on fire . . . I often heard anti-German shouts . . . many times, on seeing Germans, they shouted 'out with the foreigners' . . . I also saw them applauding a bonfire of Fascist insignia.[5]

Unfortunately, the jubilation was short lived as Badoglio's new Government announced that it would remain at war on Hitler's side. Essentially this was a diversionary tactic. The new Prime Minister secretly entered immediately into direct negotiations with the Allies. It was fairly obvious to all observers – the Roman citizens, the diplomats and indeed the Germans – that this was what he intended to do.

The situation here is still extremely delicate. There are now twelve German divisions in the peninsula and six more on the way . . . Three divisions in the neighbourhood of Rome are causing anxiety as it is feared they may seize both the King and the Pope in case of capitulation. 'We regret' said a cabinet member to me today 'that the Allies have not a clearer comprehension of our painful situation. The forces are still four hundred miles away yet they want us to capitulate and at the same time fight the Germans. We are not in a position to continue fighting but we are unable to withdraw from the conflict. All our people are disappointed that peace did not follow immediately after the fall of Mussolini.'[6]

(*MacWhite*, 11 August 1943)

Indeed, after the War it emerged that on 29 July German code breakers listened to a telephone conversation between Churchill and Roosevelt on the topic of an Italian Armistice. The new Italian Government was playing for time because they were aware that they did not have the forces to resist any German occupation. However, they exaggerated the possibilities that were open to the Allied Forces. They thought that the Allies could occupy Rome quite rapidly. However, a US General, Maxwell Taylor, went behind enemy lines to consider the possibilities of an air drop to secure Rome. He met Badoglio in Rome on 8 September but quickly realised that an air drop would not be sufficient to establish control of the city and he advised his Commander, Eisenhower, accordingly. Within the Vatican, D'Arcy Osborne and Tittmann were of the belief that the Germans were likely to take over Rome, and possibly the Vatican, so they began to destroy all confidential documents. Indeed, on 4 August, Cardinal Maglione held an urgent meeting of all his fellow Cardinals living in Rome. He advised them that the Italian Government was expecting a German coup and an invasion of the Vatican. Government sources had predicted to him that the Germans would seize the Pope and take him to Munich.

German–Italian tension is increasing daily and anything may happen at any moment. The cordon of Italian troops in the immediate vicinity of Rome has been reinforced ostensibly against an Allied attack but in reality against the Germans who form another cordon eight or ten miles away.[7]

(*MacWhite*, 31 August 1943)

The Allies and the Badoglio Government announced the signing of the Armistice on 8 September. The German Commander, Kesselring, was taken by surprise but moved fairly quickly to take control of Rome.

An American-born nun, Mother Mary St Luke, was working in Rome at the Vatican Information Bureau. Her diary entries around that time captured the mood:

> At half past seven the news of the Armistice broke. The Roman Radio broadcast Eisenhower's statement involving Badoglio's short dignified address to the Italian people. Armistice – a sigh of relief went up from the crowds around the loudspeakers. Then a pause. People looked at each other questioningly – 'Armistice or Armageddon?' What about the Germans? In country places such as Cori, up in the hills where there were no Germans, the rejoicing knew no bounds; bonfires were lit, and the peasants and the village folk rioted to their heart's content. But Rome was quiet. Marshal law was still in force, and by 9.30 the streets were deserted. But there were plenty of celebrations indoors.[8]
>
> (*Mother Mary St Luke*, 8 September 1943)

> In the papers there was a chorus of approval for Badoglio's measures. The German radio let loose a flood of invective against the 'vile treason of the Italians' . . . People overflowing with optimism began to talk English freely on the telephone. Yes, it was all over. The Italians would have to hold out for just one week and then the Allies would be here; they dropped leaflets to that effect. Everything was lovely . . . In the afternoon it clouded over and the morning's optimism clouded over too . . . By six, knots of people collected in the streets and the word went around in horrified whispers that the Germans were marching into Rome . . . A lot of Italian soldiers hastily put on civilian clothes. The Roman barracks were evacuated.[9]
>
> (*Mother Mary St Luke*, 9 September 1943)

By midday St Peter's was shut. When, in the memory of man

had it been shut in the daytime? . . . At the Arco delle Campane gate a Swiss with business-like rifle and bayonet instead of his medieval pike, guarded the entrance . . . By degrees the fighting moved in from the country . . . and near St Paul's Italian soldiers appeared in disorder, straggling along the Lungotevere, dusty, hungry and bedraggled. But there were no officers. The men reported that their officers said 'we have no more ammunition. Do what you can for yourself, boys,' and left them . . . the whole thing was a mixture of riot, civil war, real war and anarchy.[10]

(*Mother Mary St Luke*, 10 September 1943)

T. J. Kiernan describes the atmosphere in Rome from his perspective:

During the forty days of the Badoglio Regime, Rome was a city of the wildest rumours. One day it was declared 'an open city. The next day it was not. The Allies were reported to have made a landing at Ostia, the seaside resort of Rome. They had not. And so the rumours went round and round while German Battalions advanced towards the city . . .[11]

De Wyss, the journalist, had similar experiences:

People were excited and depressed in turn. They feared the Germans more than ever, which is right, I suppose. All Italians I talked to asked angrily: 'but where are the Allies? But what are the Allies doing? Why are they not coming here?'[12]

Some time later MacWhite observed the scene:

Fighting continued through the day. At 5.00 p.m. German tanks came around the corner of the Grand Hotel and proceeded towards the railway station two hundred yards away which was occupied by the Italians who after a half hour cannonading withdrew . . . situation is very confused. Romans are praying for a rapid arrival of the Allies. The King and cabinet . . . have left the city for an unknown destination.[13]

(*MacWhite*, 11 September 1943)

Meanwhile, Mother Mary was quick to note the changing circumstances in the city.

> At 1 o'clock the Roman radio now German-controlled of course, broadcast the following 'Yesterday an armistice was agreed upon by the commanders of the German and Italian troops in the area. Since then the behaviour of Italian soldiers has been such that the following measures have been taken.
>
> 1. It is forbidden to carry arms. Soldiers bearing them will be arrested and disarmed.
> 2. Anyone killing a German soldier will be shot. Otherwise the armistice remains in force.
>
> So was it an armistice. Or wasn't it?[14]
>
> (*Mother Mary St Luke*, 11 September 1943)

Indeed, as Mother Mary had observed, the Germans were in fact in control of the city by that date. Hitler went on Radio Rome to make an address to the Italian people. This address made it clear that the German authorities would introduce a regime which would make the Italians pay dearly for having deposed 'her greatest son . . . since the fall of the ancient world'. Immediate arrangements were put in place to imprison Italian military personnel. By 11 September, Kesselring was in complete charge of Rome and issued a proclamation which, among other things, stated the following:

> 1. The Italian territory under my command is declared to be a war territory. It is subject throughout to the German martial law.
> 2. Any crimes committed against the German armed forces will be judged according to German martial laws.[15]

Later on in the document further regulations were outlined:

> 6. Until further notice, private correspondence is suspended. All telephone conversations should be as brief as possible, and they will be strictly supervised.
> 7. Italian civil authorities and organisations are responsible to me for the maintenance of public order. They will prevent all acts of sabotage and of passive resistance to German

measures, and they will co-operate fully with the German organisations.[16]

Less than 24 hours after Hitler's address, the Germans managed to snatch Mussolini from captivity and he was subsequently moved to Lake Garda where he set up a government which had no real power, merely acting as a front for the German occupation.

The senior German diplomat in Rome at that time was Ambassador von Weizsaecker who, in fact, was not a Nazi. In his own mind, the Ambassador hoped somehow to organise a situation where the Vatican might mediate a peace between the Allies and Germany. Ambassador von Weizsaecker was authorised to inform the Pope in mid-September that the Germans would respect the independence of the Vatican and would protect the Vatican City from fighting.

At that stage there were about 80,000 Allied servicemen and civilians opposed to the regime imprisoned in 72 camps and 12 hospitals throughout Italy. The desertion by the Italian guards in camps all around the country enabled approximately 50,000 prisoners of war to gain their freedom. Of these, 18,000 were not recaptured in the succeeding months. This situation created a new challenge for O'Flaherty: not only were the numbers seeking help increasing greatly but the Germans had now established a military government and the Gestapo became more influential in the security situation throughout the city. Clearly a more formal, secure and organised approach was now necessary. O'Flaherty decided to look for help from the British authorities and so approached D'Arcy Osborne with whom he had developed a friendship on the golf course over the years. Given that so many of those whom he was likely to be assisting were British, the Monsignor was fairly confident of a positive response but the Minister took a very formal position. The British Minister was aware that he was being watched and needed to be very careful to avoid compromising his own role and that of the Vatican authorities. He had adverted to this issue previously in his diary:

> I believe that daily reports are sent out on our doings. They must be dammed dull reading. The precise connection

between the Italian police outside and the Vatican plain clothes police and gendarmerie inside defies precise definition but it very definitely exists. In its subtlety it is both very Italian and very Vatican. So that, while guests of the Pope, we are at the same time to some extent prisoners of the Italian Government.[17]

These concerns were shared by others. In December 1938 MacWhite wrote to Walshe advising that plain-clothes men were watching foreign diplomats and that he had heard that even diplomatic pouches were being tampered with regularly.

Certainly there were close links between the Vatican gendarmerie and their Italian counterparts probably because many of those in the Vatican had previously been employed in the Roman police force outside. Over and above that of course there was always the danger of agents working inside the Vatican and passing on information. So, while D'Arcy Osborne took the view that he could not get involved, he acknowledged that the Monsignor had offered great assistance to his countrymen and in return he made a promise to provide funds from his own personal resources as distinct from official ones. Far more importantly, however, he suggested to O'Flaherty that it might be useful for the Monsignor to have a discussion with the Ambassador's man-servant, John May. May proved to be a most valuable ally. Indeed O'Flaherty subsequently described May as 'indispensable, a genius, the most magnificent scrounger I have ever come across'.[18]

The man-servant had a particular talent in using the black market, which was to prove invaluable in the months ahead. He also had a range of contacts which kept him very well informed in relation to events on the ground. There are even suggestions that he used bribery, from time to time, to great effect in his ongoing work with O'Flaherty. It became clear when May and the Monsignor had this conversation that the Englishman was already well informed of O'Flaherty's activities. He strongly impressed on the Monsignor the need to share the burden:

'Look, Monsignor, this thing is too big for one man, you can't handle it alone . . . and it has hardly begun! Oh, I know you have got every 'neutral' Irish priest in Rome helping you, everyone knows that. And there are the others, those Maltese, that big New Zealander, Fr Sneddon, isn't it? Well, excuse me Monsignor, but they are only priests. I mean they don't know their way about like I do, and some of my . . . er friends.'[19]

As a direct result of this discussion, a Council of Three was established, consisting of O'Flaherty, May and Count Sarsfield Salazar of the Swiss Legation. Because of his position as a diplomat from a neutral country, Salazar was in an ideal position to contribute to the work of the group. Many of those who came to Rome seeking help approached the Swiss Legation. The British Embassy at this stage had been closed since the staff had moved into the Vatican but the building was under the care of Secundo Constantini, another Swiss with whom Salazar had close links. Aside from passing on information to O'Flaherty about those who were seeking assistance, Salazar's main role was to ensure that money and other resources such as food and clothing reached those hidden in the countryside around Rome. Captain Leonardo Trippi was another strong supporter at the Swiss Legation where he worked as Military Attaché issuing Red Cross parcels and generally supporting those who came seeking assistance. There was not much about prisoners and prisoners of war that he did not know as he had spent a lot of time visiting Italian camps on behalf of his own Government which was the neutral power under the Geneva Convention. As well as the Red Cross parcels he supplied money to escapees for which they would sign and which the Swiss authorities charged up to the British Government.

4

A Clerical Coalman

Early clients of the group were French soldiers who arrived at the British Embassy where they were met by Constantini. He in turn contacted O'Flaherty who went to seek accommodation for them. By chance, on the street he met an acquaintance of his, a Maltese priest, Fr Borg, who suggested that a countrywoman of his, Henrietta Chevalier, might be able to help. This episode was the first of many involving the Maltese woman. Indeed her contribution to the work of the Council of Three for the remainder of the War was quite extraordinary.

Mrs Chevalier was a young widow with six daughters and two sons. Her eldest son was imprisoned as soon as Italy entered the War because, being Maltese, he was a British subject. Her second son, Paul, was a clerical officer with the Swiss Legation and so his diplomatic papers protected his freedom. He also lived at the Legation. The youngest daughter, aged nine, was sent to live with Maltese nuns in Rome because of the dangerous situation in the city. This left Mrs Chevalier, her mother and her five remaining daughters, ranging in age from twenty-one to thirteen, living in a small third-floor apartment on the Via dell Impero.

Paul rang home at about lunchtime and spoke to his sister Rosie and asked her to 'tell Mama that I am bringing home two books'. Neither his sister nor his mother understood what the message meant. However, later in the afternoon, he turned up with two French soldiers whom, he told his mother, he had brought to her at the request of Fr Borg and she should expect a visit from a Monsignor friend of the Maltese priest that evening. O'Flaherty, when he arrived, explained the dangers involved for the Chevaliers if they were to hide the Frenchmen. Similar warnings were given by the Monsignor to Mrs Chevalier on many occasions in succeeding months, all to no avail. The apartment in which her family lived consisted of two bedrooms, a dining room, a kitchen, a box room, a bathroom with toilet, another toilet on the back balcony and a large larder. To cater for the visitors the dining room became a bedroom at night. Mattresses were laid on the floor each night and this practice continued for much of the remainder of the War as the house had innumerable guests. On one occasion there were nine overnight guests in addition to Mrs Chevalier, her mother and her five daughters. Throughout all of this time, O'Flaherty was aware of the grave dangers for Mrs Chevalier and her family as it was certain they would be executed if their activities became known. On this first occasion, he just asked that the Frenchmen be kept for a day or two as an emergency measure until he could find a more suitable location.

Mrs Chevalier and her family were involved in this work for almost all of the rest of the War. She tended to stay at home to look after her 'boys', as she called them, while her daughters went out to shop for the necessities. As soon as false papers were provided for the escapees, they were able to go out with the daughters onto the streets of Rome without arousing suspicion. However, security became of huge importance and the girls no longer brought their own friends to the house. Inevitably, in a confined block of apartments, neighbours must have known or at least suspected what was going on, but they kept their counsel. Over and above that, the caretaker of the apartment block, Egidio, and his wife, Elvira, were of great support in alerting Mrs Chevalier to any imminent danger.

Understandably, there were few locals, if any, who were willing to undertake the same level of risk as the remarkable Maltese widow. Aside from any other consideration, the dangers were obvious with an automatic death penalty awaiting anyone who assisted escapees, so O'Flaherty's next move on behalf of the Council of Three was to rent a flat on the Via Firenze. It surely delighted his sense of mischief that the apartment block backed onto a hotel used as the Gestapo Headquarters. Of all the accommodations used during this period, this was O'Flaherty's favourite. 'Faith,' he chortled, 'they'll not look under their noses.'[1] He subsequently rented another one about a mile away on the Via Domenico Chelini.

One of the early guests in the Via Firenze apartment was a British officer in the Royal Artillery by the name of Wilson whose role had been as a saboteur behind enemy lines. Wilson found himself unable to connect with a submarine that he was to meet after one such mission and so headed for Rome and the Vatican. Unfortunately for him, the Swiss Guard were now implementing the 'no admittance for escapees' policy. It seems that Wilson did not take their instructions in this regard too well and eventually they dumped him outside the Vatican boundary. He stayed there all night. Early the next morning, having been alerted by the Swiss Guard, O'Flaherty made contact with him in the Square and took him to the Via Firenze apartment where he met those already in hiding there, including some other British soldiers, a couple of Yugoslav girls and one Yugoslavian Communist, Bruno Buchner. The first thing Wilson did was sit down and write a letter to the Pope complaining about his treatment at the hands of the Swiss Guard. O'Flaherty was delighted to hand this over and equally amused some days later to deliver a reply from the Secretariat inviting Wilson to visit the Vatican at a more convenient time.

Keeping these two apartments running – paying the rent and providing food for the guests there – together with contributing to food for others who were in hiding elsewhere, began to cost significant amounts of money from the Monsignor's own resources and from other funds made available through D'Arcy Osborne, including the British Minister's own personal funds and, at this stage, Government money also. Another source of finance was Prince Filippo Doria Pamphilj, the head of one of the ancient Roman noble families, who had been a friend of O'Flaherty since before the War. The Prince was half-English and had attended university at Cambridge. During his time there he became ill and was hospitalised. One of the nurses he met was Glaswegian and he subsequently married her. Both of them had been publicly anti-

Fascist from the beginning. As often happened with O'Flaherty, offers of help came in just when they were needed. The Prince contacted O'Flaherty and, having discussed with the Monsignor the work of the Council of Three, gave him 150,000 lire. Between September 1943 and June 1944 the value of the lira depreciated by 500 per cent. This, the first of many donations which the Prince and his family gave, was worth about £2,000 at that time (the equivalent of approximately €100,000 in current terms). Sr Noreen Dennehy, a young Kerrywoman, became an unwitting transporter of these donations.

> He would bring a letter up to the convent and Mother Superior would give it to me to take down to this princess, wait for an answer and bring it back. He would come back to the convent later on and pick it up. I could never understand what was going on . . . I wasn't told anything . . . why is it that he could not go down and pick it up himself. After all he had a car. After the War was over Mother Superior did say to me one day 'You were very lucky that you weren't held up or put in jail.' I said 'what did I do' . . . 'Never mind 'tis all over now.'[2]

Mother Superior had decided not to tell the young nun that she was in fact transporting cash for fear that she might become nervous and attract attention. These donations continued even when the Prince and his family had themselves to go into hiding in Rome.

Another who found himself some time later as an unwitting transporter of cash was Fr Seán Quinlan (later Monsignor). The Quinlan family had been neighbours of the O'Flahertys in Mangerton View in Killarney and Seán remembered being carried as a child on Hugh's shoulders on many occasions. He arrived in Rome in 1938 and renewed the acquaintance. He recalls being in the Monsignor's office one day and being handed a large envelope which he was asked to bring to a particular address about a mile along the Tiber away from the Vatican. His instruction was 'to hand it over to Giovanni' and he did so. Later that evening he met Monsignor O'Flaherty who casually told him that the envelope contained one million lire. Many years later Fr Quinlan remarked that on that day he was very close to being either a millionaire or dead.

These various contributions enabled the Council to increase greatly the number of localities they could use because they were now in a position to support financially those who were accommodating the escapees. Inevitably, however, as they became more successful, the number of requests grew. This, in turn, increased the risks to O'Flaherty and his colleagues as more and more people became aware of their work. The Monsignor spent countless hours visiting the various locations in which escapees were lodged and bringing escapees to them, often ignoring curfew regulations. During the course of this work he had some narrow escapes. Indeed we will never know all the details because of his self-effacing attitude towards his work.

As time went by, the authorities gradually became aware of his activities and Kappler, the Head of the Gestapo in Rome, arranged for a watch to be kept on the houses of known associates of his, including that of Prince Doria. One day in the early autumn of 1943, O'Flaherty visited the Palazzo on the Via delle Corso where the Prince lived, to collect a contribution. The watching Gestapo officers immediately alerted Kappler who arrived with a large force minutes later. From an upstairs window in the room where the Prince and the Monsignor were talking, the Prince's secretary noticed the commotion and raised the alarm. This gave O'Flaherty a few minutes' warning of the impending search. The Monsignor immediately took his leave of the Prince, not forgetting to take the donation of funds. He had no particular plan in mind but he was aware that the Palazzo was a huge building and so presumably thought he had some chance of escape. Instinctively he went down to the basement of the house. Meanwhile the Prince's servants delayed the admission of the Gestapo for as long as they could. On arriving in the basement, the Monsignor noticed that a patch of light was shining in and quickly realised that a coal delivery was under way. The coal was being delivered from outside the house through a trapdoor directly into the cellar. Having been distracted by the activities of the Germans, the coalmen had paused in their delivery, enabling the Monsignor to climb up the pile of coal and carefully look out to assess the situation. He saw that the two coalmen were standing by the lorry and approximately two dozen of the Gestapo were about to enter the Palazzo. He managed to pull in an empty coal sack that was lying on the ground and he slid back down onto the floor. He took off his clerical outer garments, stripped down to his trousers and vest and covered himself in coal dust. Just then, one of the German officers shouted to the coalmen to complete the delivery. As one of the coalmen approached the trapdoor, the Monsignor decided to gamble on his goodwill and, attracting his attention, advised him that he was a priest who was being followed by the Gestapo. Luckily for him, the coalman agreed to assist and came down into the cellar, allowing O'Flaherty to make the return journey towards the lorry in his place. The Monsignor had on his back a coal sack containing his outer clerical garments. Presumably any SS man looking at the situation assumed he was the coalman bringing back empty sacks to the lorry. O'Flaherty managed to walk past the Gestapo, go to the lorry and then beyond and make his escape. The sacristan of a nearby church was surprised when a coalman arrived, announcing himself as a priest. However, he quickly accepted this as genuine. O'Flaherty cleaned himself up, changed into his normal clothing and headed back to the Vatican. His extensive knowledge of the back streets of Rome, which later enabled him to write a guide to the Eternal City, surely came to his assistance. We can assume that the walk which normally would take about thirty minutes was completed in far less time. Several hours later, the Prince's phone rang and he was surprised to hear the Monsignor at the other end.

> 'I am back home, are you well, me boy?' O'Flaherty said
> softly. 'Fine, now', replied Prince Doria. 'Some day you must
> tell me how you did it. I am afraid Colonel Kappler is a very
> angry man. He spent two hours here and he did say that if I
> happened to see you, I was to say that one of these days he
> will be entertaining you . . .'[3]

This very near miss led to the Council of Three taking a slightly different approach from then on, with O'Flaherty making fewer visits out through the streets of Rome and people being encouraged to come and see him, rather than vice versa. Now O'Flaherty spent evenings at the top of the steps to the Basilica saying his prayers, of course, as he was obliged to, but also being available to those who might need assistance. It was a very strategic position to take from a number of points of view. On a practical level, it would be quite easy for his colleagues and helpers to direct those in need of assistance to him as the location was prominent and O'Flaherty himself was a man of fairly distinctive features and was six foot two inches tall. In this location also, he could be observed by the German officers on duty at the boundary between Rome and the Vatican. This boundary was indicated by a white line painted along the ground linking the end of the two arms of Bernini's Colonnades. At the same time, the Swiss Guards on duty at their station at the Arco delle Campane were just a few yards from him. They were aware that the authorities were very anxious to get their hands on O'Flaherty and that if they did he would never be seen again. There was always the possibility that the Germans would cross the boundary in an effort to catch him and the Swiss Guard were on the alert to stop any such endeavour. Finally and most interestingly, O'Flaherty in this position was visible from the Pope's study.

Despite all these concerns about his safety, and all the advice he was given in that regard, O'Flaherty still regularly ventured onto the streets of Rome. He did not always use the clothes normally worn by somebody in religious life and was known to disguise himself frequently as a street cleaner. At other times, he went through the streets of Rome dressed as a labourer or a postman. Anecdotal evidence would suggest that he also, on occasion, disguised himself as a nun. (It is hardly likely that nuns over six foot tall were a normal feature of life in Rome at that time, but then again, the Germans were looking for a priest. The Germans' literal interpretation of instructions probably saved him.) This sort of activity subsequently earned him the nickname 'the Pimpernel of the Vatican'. He got help in all sorts of unusual places. He had made a practice for many years of saying an early Sunday morning mass which was availed of mainly by men who worked on the trolley-car system in Rome. These proved to be an invaluable source of support and help when he was moving escapees through Rome in subsequent years.

During this period, the Monsignor had to attend to his normal work at the Holy Office so John May kept daylight watch near St Peter's. One of the first people to approach him was a Corporal, Geoffrey Power, who arrived there one day, like so many others, with no particular plan in mind. May noticed him and took him in charge, bringing him to O'Flaherty in whose office he stayed during that day. That night, O'Flaherty brought him to the Via Chelini apartment. A few days later he was moved on to live with an Italian family for the remainder of the War.

The experience of an Irish Augustinian priest, Kenneth Madden, gives an indication of O'Flaherty's ways of recruiting people to help. Fr Madden was a young man who had been ordained in Rome in 1943. A nun who worked in one of the hospitals in Rome told him about an Italian family she knew of, living on the outskirts of the city, who were looking after a young British soldier who had escaped from a prisoner-of-war camp. The family were nervous and wanted to move this young man on. Fr Madden had known Monsignor O'Flaherty for years but had no idea of the work his fellow Irishman was undertaking. However, he knew him as a man who could be approached if one needed help and so told him the story. The Monsignor helped this family and moved the young British soldier to a safer location with Fr Madden's assistance. Soon, Fr Madden found himself deeply involved in the work. One day Monsignor O'Flaherty contacted him with a request to make a delivery to 'a few of the boys'. The delivery in fact was a caseload of medicine. Fr Madden was occupied with his duties and asked a friend of his, Fr John Buckley, to do the delivery. In this way, Fr Buckley also became an active member of the escape organisation.

The Monsignor was at his usual post on the steps one evening when he was approached by a German Jew who was living in Rome. The Jew told the Monsignor that he and his wife expected to be arrested at any time and brought back to Germany. His concern was for their small son who was only seven, and so he was seeking the Monsignor's help. He handed over to the Monsignor a very valuable gold chain and asked that the Irishman would use this to secure his son's safety.

'I have a better plan. I will put the boy somewhere safe and I will look after the chain for you. I will not use it unless I have to. I will get you and your wife new papers, Italian papers, and you can continue to live openly in Rome.'[4]

Princess Nini produced the papers and the father and mother survived in Rome until the city was liberated. O'Flaherty placed the son in safe-keeping, probably in one of the religious houses, and the family were reunited a few days after the Allies entered Rome. The gold chain was returned.

The Germans, meantime, had decided to arrest Prince Doria and his family because of their outspoken opposition to the regime, and raided the Palazzo. The Prince and his wife, together with their daughter, hid in a small room at the far end of the vast apartments. He thought they were merely delaying the inevitable and expected that they would be found but, as it happened, they were not. The Germans left, advising they would be back at seven o'clock in the morning. In the meantime the family got way. The Prince moved to live in a monastery, grew a beard and eventually was able to walk around because he fitted the role of a monk so well. The Princess and her daughter were hidden safely away by O'Flaherty in two different houses. All remained safe until the Liberation after which the Prince was made Mayor of Rome by the new Government.

At all times one of O'Flaherty's staunchest supporters was Molly Stanley. Molly had come to Italy to learn the language as a young woman. She stayed there for the rest of her life and proved to be a very valuable ally to the Monsignor because of her intimate knowledge of Rome. Molly lived with the Duchess of Sermoneta, where she was employed to act as tutor to the children. The Duchess was a friend of Monsignor O'Flaherty's and it was in her house that Molly first met him. He was in the centre of the floor, doing card tricks for Onorato, the Duchess' son, and Miss Stanley observed this with great interest as her brother was a professional magician back in England. Soon she began to help the Monsignor in his work with escapees, concentrating particularly on helping supply them with food and visiting hospitals and prisons. Molly was just five foot two inches tall which assisted her in her role as one of the Monsignor's helpers because she tended not to be noticed as she went about her business. One of the main functions which she fulfilled for the next few years was accompanying the Monsignor on his trips through Rome whether he was in clerical garments or disguised. A man on his own attracted more attention than when he was in the company of a woman, walking through the streets. The only problem for Molly was keeping up with the Monsignor's gigantic strides.

One night when he was in his usual position at the top of the steps, Molly came to O'Flaherty, notwithstanding that the curfew was in operation. She told him that one of his earliest supporters, Prince Caracciolo, had been betrayed to Kappler. The authorities were planning to raid the Prince's house that night. O'Flaherty immediately went to scrounger-in-chief John May and asked him to borrow a Swiss Guard's uniform at once. While May was off on this errand, one of the Irish priests who helped O'Flaherty was sent off to bring the Prince, warning him that he was to come immediately because there was about an hour for him to make his escape. He was brought to St Monica's Monastery, opposite the Holy Office, just yards from one of the colonnades. There he changed into the Swiss Guard's uniform. Then the Prince and O'Flaherty went to stand in what must have been, at night-time, the very stark location of the Bernini Colonnades to await the changing of the Swiss Guard. Precisely at midnight, five members of the Swiss Guard led by an officer marched through the Arco delle Campane to relieve their colleagues on duty in the historic square. As those who were going off duty marched back, they passed quite close to O'Flaherty and the Prince who, now in the full regalia of a Swiss Guard, quickly joined the marching group. As they passed near the German College he slipped into safety.

The same tactic was used some time later to assist the sister of a Vatican nobleman who was being sought by the Fascists. This time O'Flaherty used it to get her into the British Legation. At the midnight changing of the guard she joined the troop as it walked by into the Vatican property and, as the end of the marching column passed where O'Flaherty and May were hiding, the Monsignor reached out and brought her into the shadows. The Guards marched on and John May escorted her into British Legation. She remained in hiding there until the Liberation of Rome.

An Irish Guards officer, Colin Lesslie, was captured in Tunisia towards the end of March 1943. However, in September, when he was being moved for medical treatment, he managed to escape from his captors. He made his way into the Apennine mountains where a local peasant, like many of his countrymen, risked death to help the escapee. He stayed in a cottage in the mountains until the onset of winter forced him to think of other possibilities. At that stage, the local partisans introduced Cedo Ristic to the Irishman. Lieutenant Ristic Cedomir was a Yugoslav officer who was in charge of an area in the north of Italy where hundreds of escapees were in hiding, many making their way to neutral Switzerland. Ristic had some financial resources available which were used to provide Lesslie with proper clothing and a train ticket to Rome. As it was the Italians who were looking for him, not the Germans, he sat in a carriage with five SS men on the train journey and he reached the Eternal City safely on the morning of 20 October.

Instinct suggested to him that the safest place for him to stay was a church so he spent the day moving from church to church until the onset of darkness when he went into the office of the International Red Cross in the Via Sardinia where he knew Ristic worked from time to time. As it happened, Ristic was on duty and he brought him to the closed-up British Embassy which, as we know, was in the care of Secundo Constantini. Presumably because the building was closed up, the Germans kept no proper watch on the former British Embassy. Constantini kept there a supply of spare clothing and nobody ever seemed to notice that people went into the empty building in a rather ragged condition but came out well dressed. Because no watch was being kept, it was easy for Lesslie to be smuggled in, and he spent a week there. However, Constantini knew that this was a risky arrangement and it could not go on forever, so he made contact with O'Flaherty. The Monsignor called and was delighted to meet the first of his own countrymen to whom he could offer assistance. O'Flaherty

The O'Flaherty family c. 1925, l–r: Hugh, his sister, Bride, his parents, Margaret and James, and his two brothers, Jim and Neil.

Monsignor Hugh O'Flaherty playing golf to a handicap of five – very respectable for a man then in his fifties.

St Peter's Basilica and Square today.

Sam Derry.

The real Vatican identity card produced for Derry, describing him as Patrick Derry, an Irish writer employed in the Vatican.

John May – the 'most magnificent scrounger'.

Bill Simpson in 1946.

Mrs Henrietta Chevalier, the gallant Maltese widow who hid many escapees for the Rome Escape Organisation.

Monsignor Hugh O'Flaherty with Mrs Henrietta Chevalier (in the white hat) and her family, taken on her daughter Emma's wedding day.

Molly Stanley, the diminutive Englishwoman who accompanied the Monsignor on many of his errands of mercy around Rome.

Flight Lieutenant Garrad-Cole.

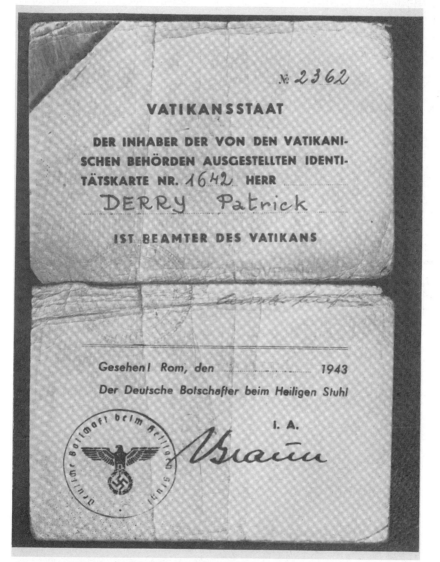

The pass which John May tricked the German Minister into issuing for Sam Derry (under his false name, Patrick Derry).

A 1930's photo of the singer, Delia Murphy.

reasoned that it would be safer to move Lesslie at night so he undertook to return at 8.00 p.m. He arrived back at the Embassy carrying the full regalia of a Monsignor. O'Flaherty himself wore the simple clothing of an ordinary priest. O'Flaherty had a small black car at the back door of the Embassy and swiftly drove Lesslie towards St Peter's Square and up to the Arco delle Campane. Then they had to face the difficulty of walking into the Vatican. The clerical disguise worked perfectly and the two passed through and made their way into the Vatican City and Hospice Santa Marta. There Lesslie was introduced to the British Minister, D'Arcy Osborne, and they were shortly joined by Harold Tittmann, the American Chargé d'Affaires. He briefed the two diplomats and the Monsignor on the situation in relation to prisoners of war in the north of Italy. After that meeting, O'Flaherty brought Lesslie to his accommodation in the German College and they sat down to a meal. As always the meal was served by one of the German nuns, causing Lesslie some confusion and concern, but he was soon reassured. The following day O'Flaherty took him to the apartment in the Via Domenico Chelini and subsequently moved him on a couple of occasions. The difficulty was that, at six foot tall, it was difficult to pass the Irish Guardsman off as an Italian, so for safety reasons he was moved to the American College. There he joined a motley crew which included fifteen American citizens of Italian extraction who had been unable to get to the US after the attack on Pearl Harbour, eight British soldiers, one American GI, two American airmen and an Italian Air Force pilot who was on the run because he had been involved in the move which led to the Italian surrender.

Lesslie was very anxious to get word back to his wife Eileen that he was safe. When he had been first captured he was aware that Eileen had been visited by the village policeman and told that her husband had been killed in action. She had subsequently learned that he was in fact a prisoner of war but after that, when he escaped again, he was reported to have been killed. John May devised a simple mechanism for getting word back to Eileen: Lesslie was asked to write a cheque for £5 on a plain piece of paper to which May affixed a stamp. May sent the cheque through the

Vatican diplomatic bag to his bank in Palmer's Green in London. A few days later Mrs Lesslie got a message asking her to visit her own bank manager at Lloyds in Old Bond Street where she was shown the cheque and of course was able to identify the handwriting. This very ingenious and simple way of getting word back home was used over and over again to reassure families.

O'Flaherty's link man in the American College was Monsignor Joseph McGeogh. US Government funds were channelled through Tittmann to aid the prisoners in hiding there. Initially Tittmann took the view that the American operation would be independent but as the months went by he soon found that he had to rely more and more on O'Flaherty and the care of American escapees was handled in the same way as all the other Allies. Mother Mary in her diary charted the changing circumstances in the city:

> More and more people are hiding, moving their lodgings or taking to the hills. It is still warm and mild, and the allies are expected here shortly – but suppose they delay. The people in the hills will die of hunger and exposure.[5]
>
> (*Mother Mary St Luke*, 21 September 1943)

> We are burying our valuables, having a nice little garden which will afford scope for such activities. We buried them darkly, after supper, aided by a small electric torch until somebody said: 'Douse the glim' for fear of neighbours watching us.[6]
>
> (*Mother Mary St Luke*, 23 September 1943)

> All men born in 1921, '22, '23, '24 and '25 are called up for 'labour service' which means they will either be taken to Germany or be put to building and repairing roads and digging trenches for the Germans in Italy; they are to present themselves at the Labour Office at once. Of course, no one intends to do so . . . The Fascists are coming forward in the pose of saviours of the people saying that they are 'the buffer between the Germans and the populace'. They have re-established the headquarters of the Roman Group, the Fascio Romano at Palazzo Braschi . . . Some truculent looking

youths with black shirts and rifles were lounging in the doorway today when I passed there, and the bunting was all hanging down, disconsolately in the September drizzle. The press says 'The old Fascist offices are in full activity, combatants, Party members and the Roman people are all flocking to them'. There was very little flocking this morning.[7]

(*Mother Mary St Luke*, 24 September 1943)

More orders have been published, with added emphasis, that those called up for labour service MUST present themselves at once. So far, out of the three thousand who should have joined up in the City of Rome, sixty have put in an appearance.[8]

(*Mother Mary St Luke*, 27 September 1943)

We are constantly asked to suggest possible hiding places for the men who are trying to escape from military and labour service with the Germans. Everyone seems to be in hiding. Some of the Germans are deserting and trying to hide also; they are mainly Austrians. The common soldiers are sick and tired of the war but not the officers.[9]

(*Mother Mary St Luke*, 3 October 1943)

The ordinary routine detail of daily life was also becoming difficult:

Almost all shops and cafes are closed as they have no stock. All motor vehicles including taxis and buses as well as horses and mules have been requisitioned. Thousands of young men have fled to the hills to escape conscription.[10]

(*MacWhite*, 9 October 1943)

In July 1938, the Mussolini Government had published its 'Manifesto of the Race' in which Italian Jews were referred to as 'unassimilable aliens'. This was followed by the introduction of a number of anti-Jewish laws and regulations. They first made it illegal for Jews to study or teach in any Italian school or university and ensured that books written by Jewish authors were removed from all libraries. Hundreds of Jews were sacked from their jobs in various branches of the Civil Service, the universities and other professions. As it happens, the Jewish community in Rome had made a huge contribution to its intellectual life. Many of its leading university professors were Jewish and approximately 100 of these lost their occupations as a result. It was also required that all non-Italian-born Jews should leave the country. This particular requirement had not been implemented in the intervening years. However, during the summer and autumn of 1943, the Jewish community became a particular target for the increasingly strong German authorities.

Von Weizsaecker, the German Ambassador, and his second-in-command Kessel, who was fairly outspoken in his anti-Nazi views, met in mid-September to discuss the likely fate of the Jews living in Rome. They agreed that the outlook was extremely serious and they arranged to warn the Jewish community through a third party. The Swiss journalist de Wyss notes 'hundreds of rumours about the coming persecutions . . . the population is half crazy... Everybody is in a cold sweat.'[11]

Unfortunately, the leaders of the 12,000-strong Jewish community in the city treated this warning and these rumours with some scepticism. The Jewish community in Rome had not suffered the same sort of persecution as had occurred elsewhere which created a false sense of security. However, the diplomats' concern was well founded. Himmler had issued an instruction to Kappler, the Head of the Gestapo in the city, to proceed with the arrest and deportation of the Jews of Rome. There is some evidence that Kappler was not happy to receive this instruction, not for reasons of sympathy with the Jewish community, but because he felt it was a politically stupid step to take. Also, he doubted whether he had enough men available to him to carry out this exercise and he anticipated that the non-Jewish population would be very hostile to such action. However, he did meet the leaders of the Jewish community on 26 September and demanded 50 kg of gold. They were given 36 hours to raise this and told that if they were not successful 200 Jews would be deported to Germany. This may have been Kappler's way of circumventing Himmler's instruction but it clearly left the leaders of the community with a difficulty. By Tuesday 28 September the gold had been collected with assistance from the Vatican on the instructions of the Pope. The gold was transmitted to Berlin. However, the authorities in Berlin were not happy and orders were issued that their original instructions must be implemented. Plans were put in place to round up Jews on 16 October starting at 5.00 a.m., one hour before sunrise. Ultra intercepts recently released make it clear that the Allies were well informed about what was happening because Kappler's report, made around midnight on that day, of the actions he had taken, came into Allied possession immediately:

> Action against Jews started and finished today in accordance with a plan worked out as well as possible by the office . . . Participation of the Italian police was not possible in view of unreliability in this respect, as only possible by individual arrests in quick succession inside the 26 action districts. To cordon off whole blocks of streets, in view both of [Rome's] character as an open city and of the insufficient number of German police 365 in all, not practicable. In spite of this 1,259 persons were arrested in Jewish homes, and taken to assembly camp[s] of the military school here in the course of the action which lasted from 0530 to 1400 hours. After the release of those of mixed blood, of foreigners including a Vatican citizen, of the families in mixed marriages including the Jewish partner, and of Aryan servants and lodgers there remain 1,002 Jews to be detained.[12]

Kappler further reported that the attitude of the Italian population was one of passive resistance but noted that a large number of instances had occurred where members of the community made more active efforts on behalf of their Jewish neighbours. On Monday 18 October the captured Jews were sent to concentration camps in Germany. Mother Mary comments:

> The SS are doing exactly what one expected, and at 4.30 a.m. today began to round up the Jews in their own houses. The Rabbi did not destroy his registers and they know where every Jew lives . . . it is a nameless horror.[13]
>
> (*Mother Mary St Luke*, 17 October 1943)

This appalling episode obviously had an effect on the attitudes of the local people and immediately led to an increase in the level of activity by the resistance movement. In response to this, a new group was set up by the authorities under the leadership of a half-German/half-Italian called Pietro Koch who took charge of a group known as the 'special police unit' which became the most ruthless and effective anti-partisan Fascist organisation in Rome.

5

Sam Derry

The demands on the Council of Three and their helpers were increasing by the day. At the same time, the security situation in Rome was becoming tighter. It became clear to the three and indeed to D'Arcy Osborne who was their 'off the record' adviser that some additional organisational skills were needed to ensure the continued effectiveness of the escape line. In effect, they needed a Chief of Staff. As happened so often with O'Flaherty, just when he needed assistance an opportunity presented itself.

Sam Derry was a member of the Royal Artillery. He had been one of the thousands who escaped at Dunkirk and had been subsequently transferred to North Africa where he found himself captured at the beginning of 1942. He managed to make an escape on that occasion but was captured again – ironically by the same German unit – the following July. He was subsequently imprisoned in the Chieti Camp in Italy. He was not long there when he was invited to join the escape committee. In the spring of 1943, there had been a leak of information to the authorities in the camp and a lot of senior people who were members of the escape committee were removed to another camp. As a result, Derry, although not long there and fairly junior, ended up in charge of the escape committee and very soon there were no fewer than six escape tunnels under construction. Whenever one was discovered, another was started. Soon he was moved also. However, before he left Chieti he had organised a number of successful escapes for colleagues.

Derry had guessed correctly that Sulmona, the new prisoner-of-war camp he had been moved to, was only a staging post and that ultimately he and his colleagues would be transferred to Germany. Accordingly, he was not too surprised when a number, including himself, were ordered to march to the railway station. On the journey through northern Italy he managed to jump from the train, on the spur of the moment, and make his escape. Escapes like this were quite common during the War but obviously were fairly hazardous. Aside from the risk of being shot by the guards when jumping off the train, there was the danger of serious or fatal injury in the fall. In any event, Derry survived and eventually located a peasant smallholding that he kept under observation the following day. He realised his only hope was to throw himself on the mercy of the occupants who were an elderly couple with no English. Derry had very little Italian. However, by a judicious use of the odd word and plenty of sign language, it became clear they were willing to accommodate him and he spent the night in their barn. At this stage, he had no idea where in Italy he was but the next morning, surveying the scene, he realised he was within sight of Rome. On that day also, his host managed to make it clear to him that there were others like him in the general locality and at nightfall two local youths came to him and guided him to a warren of caves where he met a group of his fellow countrymen who were being assisted by the locals. While they were being fed and protected by the locals, it was obvious to Derry that, with the onset of winter, living in the caves was not a realistic proposition and he decided he would have to seek assistance. When he went back the next night to meet the group he found that others had joined them and there were now about 50 British soldiers, 120 miles behind enemy lines. He decided that the only feasible plan was to head for Rome in the hope that he might be able to make contact with some British diplomat. Again, by a mixture of sign language and the odd Italian word he conveyed to the elderly couple who were looking after him that he wanted to meet the local priest. On meeting him, he asked the priest to arrange for a message to be conveyed to 'anybody English in the Vatican'. He addressed a letter 'to whom it may concern' and signed it 'S. I. Derry, Major', and conveyed the fact that there was a group in urgent need of financial assistance and clothing. On the third day, the priest returned and handed over to Derry 3,000 lire (the equivalent of £12 at that time or over €600 in current terms). He had just one request, which was that the Major would provide a written acknowledgement that the money had been handed over. This the Englishman happily did, but in his written acknowledgement of the money he also requested more. Just four days later the priest returned again and handed over another 4,000 lire and this time requested Derry to meet the priest's superior. When Derry asked who his superior was, the priest was evasive. Despite this, the Major decided that he had no choice. The priest arranged for a smallholder, named Pietro Fabri, who delivered vegetables to Rome two or three times a week, to pick up the Major early one November morning. The group consisted of Fabri, the Major and one of Fabri's daughters. Before they reached the city boundary where there was a checkpoint, Fabri gestured to the Major to take cover and so he found himself under a pile of cabbages. The farmer was well known to the guards as a regular delivery man and so they passed through the checkpoint without any difficulty. Near the markets, Fabri brought the Major to a door, rang the bell and introduced him to a man named Pasqualino Perfetti. There was another man in the room by the name of Aldo Zambardi who informed Derry that he had been sent there to meet him. Less suspicious clothing was required for Derry which Zambardi provided, including his own overcoat.

> I changed then and there, and the result was rather bizarre. The trousers flapped above my ankles, the coat did not reach my knees, and the little cap sat quaintly on the top of my head. However, the two Italians seemed satisfied with the transformation, so there was no reason why I should complain, and I set off with Zambardi down the street, knowing that at least I looked nothing whatever like an English Officer.[1]

The two then got on a tram and Derry obeyed Zambardi's instructions to pretend to doze through the trip so as not to find himself drawn into conversation. Included among the passengers on the tram were some German and Fascist officers so Derry, as he said himself, tried to make himself small, no easy feat at six foot three. They alighted from the tram just beside the Ponte Vittorio Emanuele II, one of the bridges across the Tiber, and Derry enjoyed his first clear view of St Peter's. He followed Zambardi, keeping his gaze firmly on the ground to avoid catching the eye of any of the German soldiers who were in the general area, as they approached St Peter's Square. Soon he could see a very tall, lone figure in the Square wearing a long, black robe standing just outside the left-hand side of St Peter's Basilica. Derry had a feeling that this priest was watching them, although he seemed to be in prayer. Zambardi led the Major straight up to the priest who immediately turned away with the instruction 'Follow me – a short distance behind' and all three proceeded without breaking step. However, Derry became alarmed when the priest, rather than lead them towards the Vatican where he thought he would be safe, walked away and into a narrow side street. After walking a couple of hundred yards they turned into a wide, arched entrance and crossed to a massive doorway on the far side. The inscription over the door was 'Collegio Teutonicum'. Although his language skills were limited Derry knew he was heading into a German college. This, together with the turn away from the Vatican where he thought he was heading, caused him some alarm. However he had little choice but to follow on. On entering the building Derry returned the overcoat to Zambardi, who left them, and the priest led him up two steep flights of stairs along a corridor and into a small, sparsely furnished room which was divided by two long curtains. Derry was somewhat reassured to hear that this priest was the person who had sent on the money in response to his first request. In addition the offer of a nice warm bath – his first in a year and a half – was very welcome. When he returned to the room after taking his bath, it was unoccupied. Soon, a stocky, dark-haired, middle-aged man wearing a neat, black coat and pinstriped trousers entered and, in an accent containing a trace of cockney, addressed him: 'Major Derry, I believe'. The Major still did not know who he was talking to when the priest arrived back in and he introduced the middle-aged man as John May and left again almost immediately.

I looked blankly at the man named John May and asked 'does this go on all the time?' 'Pretty nearly', he laughed, 'he is an official of the Holy Office, and he has a little office downstairs, where people are in and out to see him all the time. Never seems to rest – but I expect you'll get used to that, eventually. A wonderful character, the Monsignor.' 'The what?' 'Our Irish friend – the Right Reverend Monsignor Hugh O'Flaherty.' 'Oh dear', I said, 'that sounds dammed important and I have been calling him Father all this time . . .' 'Never mind', said John May, 'the Monsignor would be the last person to worry about that.'[2]

May brought the Major up to date on the situation in relation to the British diplomatic service in Rome and the Vatican, and then left. The Monsignor returned and lunch was served by two nuns who were obviously German. After they had left, Derry felt compelled to ask 'Monsignor, are we in the Vatican?' It was explained to him that they were not quite in the Vatican but were on papal property and, as such, the German College was part of the Vatican State as distinct from the Italian one. He was also reassured as to his safety for the time being, notwithstanding the fact that it was a German college. The Monsignor then left to return to his office to do some work but returned half an hour later with a young lady whom Derry described as 'a staggeringly attractive brunette' about nineteen years old who turned out to be Blon (Blánaid) Kiernan, the daughter of the Irish Minister. There followed some conversation between the trio and it became clear that the Monsignor and Miss Kiernan were good friends (and indeed the Monsignor was a regular guest at the Irish Legation). John May returned shortly after that with an invitation to the Major and the Monsignor to join the British Minister for dinner at the Legation that night. As it happened, the Monsignor and the Major were more or less the same build so early that evening the two men, both dressed as Monsignors, left the German College and proceeded by a slightly roundabout route into a four-storey building within the Vatican walls itself. 'Not at all bad, me boy', said the Monsignor approvingly, 'you look more like a Monsignor than I do.'[3]

On the top floor of this building the Major and the Monsignor were met by John May and brought in to join the British Minister. The Minister explained that the note from Derry expressing thanks for the original 3,000 lire and his request for more had prompted Monsignor O'Flaherty, on seeing it, to think that maybe a meeting would be a good idea. In essence, over the course of that conversation it was agreed that the Council of Three would now become a Council of Four with the English Major in charge of organisational details. Derry stayed overnight in the Minister's accommodation and spent most of the next day there catching up with war news in order to be able to pass on as much information as he possibly could to those he had left in the mountains, as he had decided to return to them with further assistance and set up an organisational structure there. That evening he donned the clerical robes again and made the return journey with O'Flaherty to the German College. Looking out the window of the Monsignor's bedroom, Derry realised that they were quite close to where the British Minister was located.

> 'Didn't we go rather a long way around?' I asked wondering if it had been some sort of elaborate joke. 'We did so', he agreed, 'but the important thing is we got there and we got you back. There is a much shorter way, but it means going through two or three gendarmerie posts, where they are used to seeing me alone, and would have been suspicious of you at once. So many people go in and out of the big gates that there is far less risk of being questioned' . . . 'You think of everything' I said admiringly. 'Thinking of everything', he replied, 'is going to be your job in future'.[4]

Having stayed overnight in the Monsignor's room, Derry returned to his colleagues in the mountains in the company of Pietro Fabri, the smallholder, and passed on to them the 50,000 lire which D'Arcy Osborne had given him. D'Arcy Osborne also helped Derry set up an organisational structure. Leaving Rome was not too difficult even though there were no supplies to hide under. Guards were more careful of those coming in and did not really take any interest in those leaving. Although there were regulations as to what could be brought in and out of Rome and who could come into the city, a group leaving with an empty cart was of no interest. A few days later, again under the vegetables, he returned to Rome and the German College where he donned the Monsignor's clothes and went across to visit the British Minister. In the meantime, D'Arcy Osborne had checked out some of the background information in relation to Derry by means of a coded message which, by some unexplained means, found its way to the Foreign Office in London, then to the War Office and finally to the local police force in Newark, Nottinghamshire, where Derry was from. In this way the Minister was able to satisfy himself as to the Major's credentials and he was in a position to allow him to start work. Derry realised that his background had been checked out thoroughly. He assured D'Arcy Osborne that he was genuine and anxious to help.

> 'Quite so Major', he said, 'but you will understand I have to be very careful. The Monsignor never checks up on anybody; he simply accepts at face value everyone who asks him for assistance, and immediately gives all help he can, whatever the risk. I worry about him sometimes, but there seems to be no way of convincing him that his own life is well worth preserving. I imagine he made no attempt to check up on you?'[5]

Derry's role was to build an organisational structure on the work that the Council of Three had already undertaken, including finding places for men to live and ensuring that they regularly received food and all the necessities of life. The Minister also promised to arrange for some other officers, already availing of sanctuary in the Vatican, to provide some administrative back-up to Derry. And so, what came to be known in Government records in London as the British Escape Organisation, came into existence in late November 1943.

The administrative work involved was huge. At this stage, there were more than a thousand escapees in contact with the organisation and an early decision was made to keep as many as possible out of Rome because the risks were greatest in the city. It was also more difficult and more expensive to keep people supplied with food within the city. At the same time, future escapees, not being aware of the dangers, were most likely to drift towards Rome so a system was set up whereby they could avail of temporary accommodation before being sent out into the countryside again. Derry quickly realised that he had little chance of achieving his objectives without the assistance of the Irish Monsignor and an interesting exchange of views took place when they met later that day. Derry remarked to O'Flaherty 'It is a good thing you are pro-British, Monsignor.' This provoked a strong response when the Irishman quickly outlined his experiences, and those of his countrymen, as he was growing up. Confused, Derry then asked why the Monsignor was now being so helpful to British escapees. It emerged that O'Flaherty listened to propaganda on both sides in the early years of the War and was unsure what to believe. The experience that changed his views was the treatment of the Jews in Rome. In June 1942, the Roman newspaper *Il Messaggero* had published a photograph on its front page showing 50 or so Jews working as forced labour along the banks of the Tiber. This had been the final breaking point for O'Flaherty.

> 'Why am I helping you now? Well, I will tell you, me boy. When this war started I used to listen to broadcasts from both sides. All propaganda, of course, and both making the same terrible charges against the other. I frankly didn't know which side to believe – until they started rounding up the Jews in Rome. They treated them like beasts, making old men and respectable women get down on their knees and scrub the roads. You know the sort of thing that happened after that; it got worse and worse, and I knew then which side I had to believe.'[6]

After this clearing of the air, the two men got on well and Derry moved to live in the Monsignor's quarters at the German College. A real Vatican identity card bearing a genuine photograph of Derry was produced for him, describing him as Patrick Derry, an Irish writer employed in the Vatican. For this short period of his life, his papers described him as Roman Catholic whereas in fact he was

Anglican. These documents were enough to enable Derry to get through any routine checkpoint on the streets of Rome. However, there was always the risk that the validity of the documents would be checked by contacting the neutral Irish Legation which had a list of Irish citizens living in Rome. The authorities there would have been obliged to make it clear that there was no such Irishman in Rome as Patrick Derry. Fortunately for the Major, nobody took this step. The advent of Major Derry as an active participant in the escape organisation has an added advantage for those of us looking back at the period. In contrast to the Monsignor, he kept detailed records and he recounted his experiences in a book published in 1960 under the title *The Rome Escape Line*. This is the period of the War about which we know most in relation to Monsignor O'Flaherty.

Derry then began to introduce himself to the local organisation. He decided to visit the various locations where escapees were being catered for. This enabled him to get to know these locations but also it made him aware of the extent of O'Flaherty's network. His first visit was to the flat on the Via Firenze and he was guided there by the New Zealander, Fr Owen Sneddon. The next day he was returned to the German College and met a Fr John Claffey who was a native of County Westmeath. Fr John brought him to an apartment he shared with another Irish priest, from County Galway, Fr Vincent Treacy. Both were members of the Congregation of the Priests of St Mary and lived at the Via de Penitenzieri quite close to the Monsignor's office. Their accommodation was· very often used as a clearing house for new escapees on their arrival. Fr Claffey took Derry on to meet Br Robert Pace, a Maltese De la Salle Brother. Br Robert had a mini-organisation of his own going within the greater group at that stage, consisting of two young Italians, Sandro Cottich, a law student, and Mimo Trapani, a medical student. Br Robert introduced the Major to his gallant countrywoman, Mrs Chevalier. At that stage Mrs Chevalier had four British soldiers staying with her. Her attitude to the crucial role she played is well reflected in her comment to the Major: 'They are absolutely grand, these boys. They are just like my own children. It is all so marvellous.'[7]

Like the Monsignor before him Derry emphasised to her the dangers involved in this work. He immediately decided on a cautious strategy, whereby those lodging with her were warned that, in the event of any danger, her safety and that of her family had to come first. Others who were active in the organisation whom he met at that time were Fr Tom Twomey from Tralee and Fr Ben Forsythe from Fermoy; the Maltese Augustinian priests Fr Egidio Galea, Fr Aurelius Borg and Fr Ugolino Gatt; Fr Anselmo Musters from Holland; Fr John ('Spike') Buckley from Mayo; the Italian film director Renzo Lucidi and his wife Adrienne; Fr Madden and Fr Lenan. Among the local supporters he met at that time were Giuseppe Gonzi, Sandro Cottich, Mimo Trapani and Fernando Giustini. He was also introduced to the third member of the Council of Three, Count Sarsfield Salazar. Salazar advised that the Swiss Embassy was still being inundated with requests for help from escapees who were situated in the surrounding countryside. It was agreed that he would continue to be the channel to provide funds and other resources to them. Within a couple of days however, the Monsignor got a tip-off that the authorities were aware of Salazar's activities as he had been betrayed. The Count had to go into hiding which was just as well because a raid was carried out on the Embassy some days later. However, he continued his work for the organisation from his new location in hiding.

In the next few weeks Derry got to know other helpers of O'Flaherty's including the Pestalozza family, Prince Caracciolo, the Irish Br Humilis, a Franciscan monk at St Isidore's, and another valiant priest from New Zealand, Fr Flanagan. Br Humilis was bursar to his community and, over the years, had become expert in turning the operation of the black market to their advantage. He now brought this expertise to the O'Flaherty organisation, buying food and provisions for the various escapees in large amounts. He quickly located a farmer with a false-bottomed cart who helped to effect deliveries, and was in charge of the expenditure of significant amounts of money, running into millions of lire in the next few years. Derry was brought to most of these billets by Monsignor O'Flaherty and he recalls those events:

If the distance was reasonable we walked, partly because I needed the exercise, but chiefly because the Monsignor liked walking. In any case, tram journeys were always worrying because sometimes a voluble Italian wanted to talk, and my 'dozing' act was not invariably successful.[8]

He was lost in admiration for what had been achieved already by O'Flaherty and his colleagues.

Tramping around Rome with him, I marvelled at how his organisation had so far concealed more than a thousand ex-POWs in convents, crowded flats, on outlying farms.[9]

6

More Volunteers

As well as Princess Nini, the organisation now had another expert in producing counterfeit documents, a mysterious German lady, known only as Mrs K, who concentrated on producing bread coupons which enabled the organisation to purchase directly from the bakeries at prices cheaper than the going rate on the black market. A Madam Bruccoleri was a widow working in the Red Cross organisation in Rome. Letters which arrived in Italy from families of British prisoners of war, whether they were still incarcerated or in hiding, would come to the Red Cross in Rome. Mrs Bruccoleri was kept up to date by O'Flaherty on all those whom the organisation was catering for, so when she came across a letter regarding one of them she would slip it into her clothing and her daughter Josette would deliver it to O'Flaherty the next day. This way, those in hiding within the city and outside were kept in touch with home.

The Major also met some of the French diplomatic representatives. As we have seen, the Ambassador, Bérard, had no sympathy with the Allied cause. By contrast, the First and Second Secretaries, Jean de Blesson – who had lost all his family property to the Germans – and François de Vial were very much supporters of the Free French movement and de Gaulle. A similar situation existed in the Irish Embassy where the Irish Minister Thomas Kiernan was obliged to follow the Irish Government policy of strict neutrality while his wife, the noted singer Delia Murphy, and their daughter Blon, were free agents and very much active supporters of O'Flaherty.

It was quite natural that Kiernan's wife, Delia Murphy, and Monsignor O'Flaherty would become friends shortly after her arrival in Rome. They were two of a kind: gregarious, outgoing and sociable. It was because of Hugh of 'the twinkling eyes', she explains, that she began to get involved in helping the escapees:

> For a time I wrestled with my conscience and prayed for guidance about what I should do to help Fr O'Flaherty. A voice inside me said charity was something God intended for all humanity, in war and peace, I remembered the words of St Paul: Now abideth faith, hope and charity, these three; the greatest of these is charity. What else could it be but charity to help those in trouble with the Nazis? Around the city during the nine month occupation of Rome, the Germans had splashed posters warning that anyone found sheltering an Allied prisoner of war would be shot. I doubt if they would have shot the wife of the Irish Minister, but they might not have hesitated with others in our group . . . I made sure none of the high-ranking German warlords who invited the Kiernans to their feasts, ever suspected what an Irish woman in Rome was doing in her spare time.[1]

A very intriguing incident which involved Delia was the case of a German soldier whom an Italian had found exhausted near one of the bridges across the Tiber. This German soldier claimed to be a priest and explained he was fasting in the hope that he would be able to say Mass if he found someone who was in a position to assist him. Delia Murphy brought the German to Monsignor O'Flaherty and as soon as they were satisfied that his claim was genuine they arranged for him to say Mass. As Delia observed:

> As I watched him slowly mount the steps to God's altar I wondered about the foolishness of war and the sacrifices of life. Say what you like, I am sure if women were allowed to rule the world, there would be no more wars.[2]

Another well-known episode involving Delia Murphy was the case of the disappearing boots. Aside from money and food, the most pressing need of those who were on the run was proper footwear. Many of them were travelling long distances by foot, moving from place to place outside of Rome. In his usual way, John May identified a likely source. He discovered that a building which backed on to the garden of the Irish Legation had been taken over by the Germans and was turned into a depot where they repaired boots for their personnel. The boot depot was not guarded at night. Presumably the authorities did not anticipate trouble. For a number of weeks, boots began to disappear and were thrown over the wall into the back garden of the Irish Legation where they were subsequently gathered and passed on to O'Flaherty. Delia Murphy was certainly involved in this, by her own account, and most probably was assisted by her daughter Blon. Br Humilis comments on Delia Murphy's motivation and indeed, his own, in helping O'Flaherty.

> She did it for humane reasons to save lives. That was my thinking too, because it made no difference to me if they were German or English. I did it to save lives.[3]

During all of this time, of course, her husband was attending to his routine diplomatic duties. In November 1942 he wrote to John Charles McQuaid, the then Archbishop of Dublin, assuring him that the authorities were respecting Vatican property in the appropriate manner. He addressed this issue again in November 1943 when he reported back to the authorities in the Department of External Affairs.

> I attach a photo of the German patrol on the demarcation line between the Vatican City and Italy. There have never been more than two sentries, who halted all German soldiers and military cars and cycles and turned them back. They have not interfered with other people, who are stopped by the Swiss Guard or Vatican police from entering the Vatican or the Basilica unless they have Vatican passes.[4]

D'Arcy Osborne assigned to Major Derry some military personnel who had already secured sanctuary in the Vatican to support him administratively, most particularly a Captain Henry (Barney) Byrnes of the Royal Canadian Army Service Corps. Derry and

Byrnes immediately set up a record-keeping system. Derry anticipated that as the organisation was beginning to spend significant amounts of British Government money, it was likely, at some stage, that he would be asked to account for it. Byrnes kept these records and buried them each night in the Vatican Gardens. Money continued to be supplied by O'Flaherty's traditional supporters among the nobility and the wealthier citizens of Rome, but more and more funds were now coming from the US and British Governments through Tittmann and D'Arcy Osborne.

Inevitably because of the military involvement, the work of the organisation strayed into espionage. Derry took careful steps to make sure that O'Flaherty was not involved, for fairly obvious reasons. However, in this aspect of the ongoing work, the Monsignor's contacts throughout Rome usually meant that he had a fair idea of what was going on. British espionage agents working in the south of Italy were unaware of developments in Rome and the arrangements which had been put in place to support escapees, so they decided to send one of their agents north with money to help any he might meet there. This agent was an Italian, Peter Tumiati, who when he arrived in Rome immediately sought out O'Flaherty, like so many others seeking help on reaching the city. O'Flaherty introduced him to Derry who was rather nervous, not knowing Tumiati's background. Derry was always on the lookout for agents from the German side who might be trying to penetrate the organisation. When Derry expressed these concerns to the Monsignor the reply he received was, 'why me boy, I know him well.'[5]

Not only did O'Flaherty know Tumiati but he knew precisely what his role was. Tumiati brought back to his authorities in the south of Italy a list of all those ex-prisoners whom O'Flaherty's organisation now knew to be at large, amounting to 2,000 or so. For security reasons, the list was in the form of microfilm, organised by John May, which was secreted in a small loaf. One night a couple of weeks later, Derry was able to hear on a BBC broadcast a coded phrase that confirmed to him that Tumiati had got through with the list. This enabled the British authorities to notify the families of the 2,000 that they were 'missing – known to be safe'.

By now, finances were well organised and regular supplies of significant amounts were coming through D'Arcy Osborne, with lesser amounts from Harold Tittmann and others. A hundred thousand lire a week (approximately €15,000 in current terms) was now going through the organisation to those in hiding. In order to support the organisation, D'Arcy Osborne needed to have large sums of money available to him. The Foreign Office in London gave the Vatican bank a guarantee that it would cover any borrowings he made up to a maximum of three million lire. Major Derry had also ensured that the people involved in the work of the organisation became more security conscious. At that stage in Rome, phone calls were routinely monitored by the authorities. As we have seen, O'Flaherty had a fairly casual approach to these matters, using only the code word 'golf clubs' to refer to escapees and 'breviary' to refer to accommodation. Derry changed all that, assigning code names to the main participants including O'Flaherty himself (Golf), Derry (Patrick), Fr Claffey (Eyerish), Fr Lenan (Uncle Tom), Fr Musters (Dutchpa), Mrs Chevalier (Mrs M) and Br Robert Pace (Whitebows – referring to the two white ribbons worn by members of the De la Salle teaching order). Fr Aurelius Borg was known as 'Grobb', Fr Sneddon as 'Horace', Fr Madden as 'Edmund', Fr Galea as 'Sailor', Renzo Lucidi as 'Rinso' (then a brand name for a washing-up powder). For some unfortunate reason Count Salazar was assigned the nickname 'Emma' and Fr Flanagan, 'Fanny'. Fr John Buckley already had the nickname 'Spike' which referred to his prowess as an athlete in his younger days, when he used spiked running shoes. Other code names were given to John May (Giovanni), D'Arcy Osborne (Mount), Secundo Constantini in the Swiss Legation (Sek) and Hugh Montgomery who worked as Secretary to D'Arcy Osborne was known as Till. In the case of the locals their Christian name usually sufficed as a codename with the exception of Fernando Giustini who was known as the 'Schoolmaster' and Giuseppe Gonzi whose codename was 'Mr Bishop'.

At that stage, however, Derry's main security concern was O'Flaherty himself.

The Monsignor, needless to say, welcomed every new arrival

with cheerful enthusiasm and paid no attention to my repeated protests that he was putting himself in danger.[6]

The Monsignor continued to take enormous risks with his own personal safety going through the streets of Rome and visiting, of all places, the notorious Regina Coeli prison. In an interview carried out in 1994 by Frank Lewis for Radio Kerry, Sam Derry recalled the problems created for him in trying to ensure the Monsignor's safety.

> It was quite difficult. He was so charming and for his own safety he couldn't care a damn . . . he still kept going around Rome although he had been told not to go out. He used to disappear and it was a great problem as far as I was concerned . . . he was, in my opinion, taking unnecessary risks but, of course, he accepted no orders except from his superiors.[7]

He also continued to take at face value anyone who came seeking assistance which was obviously of concern to the more security-minded Major. On 8 December 1943, the Monsignor arrived at his room where Derry was staying and announced 'another new arrival for you Patrick'. This was a face from the past for Derry (whose codename was Patrick), a Czechoslovakian Jew by the name of Joe Pollak. When Derry was in the Chieti prisoner-of-war camp, there had been a leak of information to the authorities there. The escape committee had tried to identify the source without success. Derry's own suspicion fell on a prisoner named Joe Pollak though he had no hard and fast information. So now, when the Monsignor introduced Pollak to him again, he was quite surprised but more particularly he was concerned for the safety of everyone in the escape organisation. Derry entered into this conversation with great caution. Pollak explained that he had made for Rome, having escaped from captivity with six others. He began to name this group, mentioning first two Lieutenants, John Furman and Bill Simpson, who both had been very close friends of Derry's when they were in the prisoner-of-war camp together. These were two men whom the Major knew he could trust. More importantly he was willing to back their judgement and so he began to accept Pollak as being genuine and risk free. It was arranged that Pollak would bring Furman to meet Derry. When they met the next day, Derry managed to get Furman on his own and check out the reliability of Joe Pollak. Furman's response was 'Joe Pollak is one of the most terrific chaps I have ever met.' Furman went on to describe what Pollak had done for the escapees in the countryside, making links with anti-Fascist families who were willing to house them. Pollak's knowledge of the language had been a crucial advantage. Having heard the full story, Derry went to Pollak, whom he had left in the Monsignor's room, and made his apologies for having doubted his reliability.

The experiences of Pollak and those who came to Rome with him were fairly typical. They had gathered in the area around the prisoner-of-war camp at Sulmona, having escaped either from the camp itself or when they were being moved northwards to Germany. They were looked after by the local people there until the regularity of raids by the German authorities forced them to think of other options. Like many another group, they found Rome and the anonymity of the big city very attractive at that stage. The reality was that although he was only a Private, Joe Pollak was, in a sense, the recognised leader. Pollak's skill with languages as a fluent speaker of German, Hebrew, Greek, English and Italian was obviously of great assistance. When they were based in Sulmona, two of their supporters were Iride and Maria Imperoli. Eventually Iride went into Rome seeking help and called to St Peter's. Her objective was to make contact with a member of the British Legation staff. She had with her a letter from some of the officers seeking assistance, advice and money. A similar letter was written by the American officers in the group, Dukate and Wilson, to people in their embassy. After five days, Iride returned with a sum of 3,000 lire and the advice that Rome was not the place to which they should go. This money was distributed among those who were catering for the escapees in the general locality. A similar trip some time later yielded a contribution of 15,000 lire from the diplomats in Rome but again, the advice was not to attempt to reach the city. However, the level of the raids around Sulmona became so regular, and there were so many near misses, that the group decided they had no option but to move out. So Iride and

Maria took the group, including the Americans Elbert Dukate and Glenn Wilson, the Britons Denis Rendell, Gilbert Smyth, Furman and Simpson, and a Free French officer Henri Payonne, together with Joe Pollak, on the train to Rome. They alighted three stations outside Rome because they felt it was safer to make the rest of the journey on foot. Pollak's skill with the language and the presence of Iride and Maria helped to get them through checkpoints. Their story was that they were a family who had been bombed out of their home in Sulmona and were now making their way to their only surviving relative in Rome. When they reached the city, Iride and her sister brought them to a small hotel, the Vulcania, on the Via Cavour. The travellers were delighted with the standard of the accommodation and the availability of hot baths met with a very positive response. The receptionist showed them to their rooms.

> Upstairs, she ushered us into a spacious room. We gaped. To us it appeared elegant, the washhand basin with shining chrome taps, and a large double bed covered by a silk spread. As Iride left with the receptionist to check more rooms, each dusty face registered joyful disbelief. After prison camps and unsanitary slums, the contrast was strong. Gil ran the water 'My god, hot!', he exclaimed.[8]

It was only when they looked for food and discovered that the hotel did not provide any that they realised they were actually being accommodated in a brothel. The next morning Joe Pollak took off for St Peter's Square. After looking around for some time, he began to approach clergy for help.

> I struck it lucky with the second one. I told him about us, that I had to make contact inside. He took me across the Piazza to a side entrance, into the Holy Office building. It's 'extra-territorial' whatever that means. He went off and came back with a big tall priest called Monsignor O'Flaherty. I understand he is the important fellow in the background. He is mixed up with a whole crowd of escapers around here. He has got a British Major working with him. His name is Derry.[9]

The next day, O'Flaherty's organisation sprang into action. Dukate,

Wilson and Smyth were moved into the American College, having been taken there by car by the French diplomat, de Vial, and the rest were placed with supporters around the city. However, Furman, Pollak and Simpson quickly began to seek a more active role. As Simpson remembers it, 10 December was dark and wet when the three of them stepped off the Number 34 trolley bus. Pollak led them to a meeting with Monsignor O'Flaherty and two other countrymen of theirs, Captain Gardner, who had been a prisoner of war with them in Chieti, and Lieutenant Colonel Wilson. Furman recalls that first meeting with the Monsignor:

> He stood about Sam's height with a fine physique not much inferior to Sam's own. His face normally wore a benign, absent-minded, professorial expression, an effect which his spectacles heightened, but the mood could change very quickly and I was frequently to see the kindly twinkle in his eyes displaced by flaming passion whenever he heard of some particularly bestial cruelty perpetrated no matter by whom or against whom.[10]

Furman, Pollak and Simpson were recruited to play leading parts in the organisation from then on. Iride and Maria returned to Sulmona with fresh supplies of money for the prisoners still in hiding there. De Vial of the French Embassy managed to find temporary accommodation for the three in a flat in Rome. The following day the Monsignor and Derry sat down with their new recruits to decide on the responsibilities each would have in the restructured organisation. Essentially O'Flaherty and his army of priests, student priests and other supporters continued to do most of the work of finding new locations in which to house escapees. Furman, Simpson and Pollak took over the more dangerous work of guiding escapees to these locations, issuing money and delivering food supplies and clothes.

It is not clear whether O'Flaherty was aware that his organisation was using a brothel as a place in which to hide escaped prisoners. It might have proved very interesting to see what his reaction would have been. In a somewhat analogous situation Derry found himself in an awkward conversation with the

Monsignor one day. O'Flaherty expressed admiration for the work of one of the female members of the organisation:

> I wonder just how she does it, nobody else could hoodwink the Germans as she does. She comes and goes half the time on German lorries and I can't imagine she has deluded the drivers all this time.

Somewhat embarrassed, Derry said,

> Well, Monsignor she is a very attractive girl you know, even if a bit er . . . garish, and as a matter of fact she gets on very well with the German drivers. She, ahem . . . well she provides them with much-appreciated services that only a woman can give!
>
> O'Flaherty shot a keen glance at the slightly pink Derry and paused while the soldier wondered just how the priest would take this revelation about one of his helpers. O'Flaherty said merely, 'What a pity', and changed the subject.[11]

One of the less pleasant duties that Derry had to perform was to try to ensure appropriate levels of discipline. As the senior Allied officer in Rome he had to issue quite strong letters of admonition from time to time. So for example, a trooper named Thorpe was issued with the following:

> I have received a full report on your atrocious behaviour during the last week. I made a full report which has been sent to the proper authorities. You are to get out of Rome immediately. Immediately after liberation of Rome by the Allies you will have to answer the charges which are already serious.[12]

7

Christmas 1943

Simpson, Furman and Pollak made their first call to Mrs Chevalier on 11 December 1943 as her flat was the depot for food supplies. It was a fairly typical day in the apartment of the Maltese woman.

> 'I expected you', Mrs Chevalier smiled as we introduced ourselves. Two young girls who had been screaming at each other, fell silent. 'My daughters, Gemma and Mary' . . . two other girls appeared and inspected us. Matilda, younger than Gemma, was slim, serious and shy. The other, about twelve, was an imp . . . 'Come and meet Grandma, the seventh female in the house.' We followed Mrs M into a large kitchen, where a bright fire burned in a wide grate. A basket of vegetables and fruit stood on the floor, and large chunks of red meat lay on the table. In the corner by the window an old woman sat in a low chair peeling potatoes. Mrs M's mother, as she looked up, smiled faintly and resumed peeling. 'Some family', I said, confused. 'Oh that is not all.' She led us to another door in the corridor and pushed it open. Four men lay in one huge bed, their faces turned to us. 'Good morning', said the four in unison, as Mrs M introduced us to her four private escapers, they climbed out of bed fully dressed. 'They hop into bed every time someone comes to the door, she explained.'[1]

She went on to outline that a friend, Giovanni, provided the meat and got his friends to buy sugar and other scarce items on the black market. A baker down the street supplied the bread to her without coupons and she used the money provided by Monsignor

O'Flaherty to buy potatoes, fruit and vegetables. She explained to them that the biggest problem was delivery.

> Carrying large cases attracted attention, and the local police were alert for black marketeers. The system was hit or miss, Fr Borg and Brother Robert had taken them today. Monsignor O'Flaherty sent different people. Sometimes, when nobody arrived, two of the older girls had to step in, but it was too onerous and too risky for them.[2]

Simpson, Pollak and Furman took over deliveries the next day but they quickly found with the amount they were expected to deliver, some of it over quite a distance within the city, that the arrangements which had applied until then were impractical. From then on they secured money from Sam Derry to hire the services of a local man who had a horse-drawn carriage. This proved a more efficient way to move provisions around the city. Derry stayed in the German College. The three others had been supplied with false identity documents which were good enough to allow them to move around Rome in reasonable comfort. Each of them was described as an Italian national and all three had enough mastery of the language to get by. They moved from their temporary accommodation shortly after that to take up residence with Renzo and Adrienne Lucidi on the Via Scialoia.

Very early on in his work for the organisation, it struck Furman as curious that more of the escaped prisoners of war had not been hidden in the Vatican itself. Sam Derry explained:

> 'There are two reasons really. I will give you the one of lesser importance first. I agree it wouldn't be difficult for us to get the chaps inside, because we know how it can be done. But we only know because the Monsignor has shown us. I wouldn't be playing the game to make use of that knowledge as the Monsignor would get it in the neck from the Vatican authorities. There is a hell of an enquiry each time a prisoner gets in and you can bet that sooner or later it would be traced back to him. He is already highly suspect and we have good reason to believe he stands pretty high on the Gestapo black-list. In fact he has been warned he mustn't leave the Vatican,

but he pays pretty scant attention to the warning. The second reason is this. So far, the Germans haven't worried over-much about the Vatican. They have respected its neutrality quite reasonably. If we start filling it up with escapers there is obviously going to be a reaction.'3

Major Hugh Fane-Hervey was a Tank Commander in the North African Campaign. In June 1942, near Tobruk, his tank was hit and caught fire. His gunner was wounded and trapped in the burning tank but Fane-Hervey freed him and threw him clear. According to one witness, German soldiers who saw the incident applauded openly. Fane-Hervey was captured but subsequently escaped. He was eventually transferred to a prisoner-of-war camp at Frosinone in southern Italy. There he met Flight Lieutenant Garrad-Cole who was also captured near Tobruk. Some time later the authorities decided to transfer 25 British prisoners of war to Germany, including these two, and so they were put on a train. By this stage Fane-Hervey had managed to steal an axe which he concealed in his baggy pants and brought with him. The train stopped in Rome and remained there, stationary, for a day during which time Fane-Hervey and Garrad-Cole began to work their way through the side of the carriage which was made of timber. The following evening, when the train began to move, they continued the work and some time later clambered through onto the buffers from where they made the jump, 'a terrifying moment of hurtling through space'.4 With the help of a local shepherd and then some villagers nearby they managed to purchase train tickets to Rome. Garrad-Cole's recollection of this event illustrates clearly the workload of the organisation. It was not just a question of locating a suitable billet and ensuring food was delivered:

> I dreamed of sipping Chianti alongside unsuspecting storm troopers in a Roman café: of espionage: of beautiful Italian women. Little did I know . . . 5

In Rome, like so many more before them, they made for St Peter's:

> We looked towards the entrance to the Vatican where the Swiss Guards in their picturesque uniforms stood stolidly on

watch. We looked towards the entrance to the cathedral and saw many people entering and leaving. After a quick decision we decided to approach the first benevolent-looking priest we saw. Picking one out, we walked up to him and Fane in his best Italian, said 'We are British prisoners of war'. Just like that. The priest stopped in his tracks. His jaw dropped in amazement. He looked quickly around, but for a moment did not reply. Then gathering his wits he muttered 'I cannot help you . . . but wait here for half an hour . . . I will bring somebody who speaks English.'[6]

Eventually he came back with Secundo Constantini who was a member of the O'Flaherty organisation. He escorted them to the disused British Embassy where he and his family were living on the first floor and they stayed there for about ten days.

One day . . . we were exploring the Embassy when we came upon the Ambassador's wine cellar. It had an enormous wood and iron door which was securely padlocked and bore a Swiss Government seal. Obviously the Swiss had taken over the stocks when the Ambassador had been forced to leave and they had sealed the cellar for the duration of the war. Through a barred grille near the top of the door we could see row upon row of many different kinds of wines and liqueurs. Nearest to us, only about six feet away from the grille, was a long line of champagne bottles lying on their sides. The temptation was great, in fact too great. We foraged around until we found a good stout curtain rod and to the end of this we fixed a piece of strong cord which we tied into a slip knot. Carefully we thrust the rod through the grille until the slip knot settled over the neck of the nearest champagne bottle. Gently we removed the rod away until the slip knot was tight. Then gradually we eased the bottle off the shelf. As it dropped over the edge it nearly fell to the ground under its own weight before we were able to arrest its fall and haul it through the grille. Several other bottles followed and that night we had quite a celebration with the Secundo family who, although worried about the consequences, thoroughly appreciated the excellent wines. I have often smiled since at the thought of the head-scratching that must have gone on when the cellar was unsealed after the war, and the stock was checked.[7]

A few days later Secundo became aware that the Embassy was being watched, so Br Robert was sent to move the two Britons to a nearby Lithuanian Seminary. Again, their stay lasted about ten days when they had to be moved again because of the fear of a search being carried out. This time, they were brought to the apartment of Renzo and Adrienne Lucidi where they met three other prisoners of war, Simpson, Furman and Wilson. The apartment was too small to cater for them all, so Garrad-Cole found himself moved that evening to the French seminary. Again, some time later due to the fear of searches he was moved to live with a retired Italian Colonel and his wife on the outskirts of Rome. By this time Garrad-Cole was aware that the brains behind all of these movements was O'Flaherty, whom he had previously met when the latter visited the camp at Sulmona.

> He used to accompany the Pope's representative on visits to the camp. During these visits we used to try to get him on one side to give us the latest news on the war. Invariably he had his pockets stuffed with cigarettes which he would slip to us when the Italians were not looking.[8]

He decided to ask Br Robert to arrange for him to meet O'Flaherty. A few days later, he arrived at St Peter's and explained to the Guard Commander that he had an appointment with Monsignor O'Flaherty.

> After looking me up and down, he gave me a wink and led me down a passageway between two buildings and then into another building and up a flight of stairs to the monsignore's apartment.[9]

Garrad-Cole was surprised when he entered the apartment to find some of the escapees that he had previously met at the Lucidis' apartment.

> We had an amusing tea party and I remember that the Monsignor produced a bottle of superb cognac for us before

we left. During the course of the conversation I mentioned to him that I was living on the outskirts of Rome with an Italian Colonel, who had been most kind, but who, unfortunately, was beginning to feel the strain of hiding two prisoners in his home. 'I think I can help you' said the Irishman shaking my hand. 'I will let you know in a day or two'.[10]

Within a couple of days he was moved to live with a marchesa, who came from the north of Italy but had an apartment in Rome.

The Italian Resistance in its various forms had begun to re-assert itself and, in response, the Germans had replaced their original military Governor, Stahel, with Maelzer who took a far stronger line. On the evening of 18 December, one group of the Resistance bombed a favourite haunt of Nazis and Fascists, killing eight German soldiers. An attack was also carried out on a cinema where twice-weekly showings were exclusively for the occupying troops. On 19 Sunday, an assault was made on the Hotel Flora which was the headquarters of the German high command in the city. It is clear that there were serious numbers of casualties but the Germans kept the details secret. Immediately the curfew was changed from 11.30 p.m. to 7.00 p.m. and the use of bicycles after 5.00 p.m. was prohibited. The provision in relation to bicycles arose from the fact that one of the resistance attacks had been carried out using a bicycle as a means of transport. Notices went up on walls in Rome outlining the new regulations.

> From this moment on, without exception, the use of any bicycle anywhere in the territory of the open city of Rome is prohibited. Transgressors will be shot without regard to who they are and without prior notice.[11]

The Duchess of Sermoneta reports:

> Tricycles being allowed, the ingenious Romans added two small wheels – taken usually from perambulators – on either side of the bicycles and not quite touching the ground.[12]

After a few days these were forbidden also.

In December a new Italian Fascist police squad, under the leadership of Pietro Koch, was formed in response to the increased activity by the Resistance. Meanwhile Monsignor Montini became aware that the numbers of German security forces stationed in Rome were being increased significantly and he began to fear that an attempt to breach the neutrality of papal properties was imminent. Some days later, his fears were realised as Koch's group was used to breach the sanctuary of a number of Vatican properties.

The first target on 21 December was the seminary beside the Basilica of San Giovanni. This was the hiding place of some leading members of Italy's anti-Fascist elite. Included among these were the heads of various parties in the coalition of anti-Fascist organisations and a total of approximately 200 powerful enemies of the regime including 55 Jews. The notice on the door was the usual one on such properties, printed in Italian and German, making it clear that all searches and requisitions were prohibited because it was the property of the Vatican. Despite this, of course, such a raid was not unexpected by those in occupation and many managed to make their escape. Koch had in his group a man who had previously been a monk. Those who were caught, and pretended to be seminarians, were asked to recite the Ave Maria. This enabled the former monk to identify who were imposters. All in all, eighteen prisoners were taken. The rest managed to disperse through the city. A number of other properties were raided in the next few days. The Vatican authorities immediately made a protest but Kappler denied any German involvement when challenged by the German Ambassador, even though some of his own men had joined as part of the exercise.

The authorities then published a list of offences throughout Rome and the punishments which would apply. Anyone harbouring escaped prisoners of war, owning a wireless transmitter or not fulfilling labour obligations would be immediately executed. Anyone in contact with escaped prisoners of war, printing or publishing news derogatory to the Axis Forces, assisting with the operation of a wireless or taking photographs out of doors would be sentenced to hard labour for life. A twenty-year prison sentence would apply to anyone who failed to notify the authorities of a change of address.

It is also clear from reading Mother Mary's diary and, indeed reports from the Irish diplomats in Rome, that living conditions in the city were quite difficult. The food supply was far from satisfactory. A rationing system was in operation but even the full rations would not have been enough to meet the needs. Very often the items one was entitled to, in accordance with the rationing system, were not in fact available. There was a thriving black market but prices were very high. Kiernan wrote back to Dublin:

> The nuns prayed to St Joseph to discover black market 'bargains' and they say he answers their prayers.[13]

Later on he was to report,

> Irish priests here are not starving (except two) but they are all under-nourished as the stores they had laid in are used sparingly.[14]

Tea and coffee were more or less unavailable and bread was very scarce. The public transport system had deteriorated due to a lack of spare parts and tyres. In addition the Allied Forces had started to bomb the city.

Over the years the Monsignor paid visits home to stay with his sister whenever he got the opportunity. Also living there was his nephew and namesake, Hugh O'Flaherty, afterwards a distinguished barrister and judge, who was being cared for by Mrs Sheehan as his own mother had died when he was quite young. His aunt had very high standards as regards table settings. She was of the view that there should be two of everything, such as butter and sugar, so that nobody would have to stretch too far. Hugh (the nephew) recalls his uncle's joy at seeing such plentiful supplies which contrasted with what he had been experiencing in Rome.

Koch's gang was in many ways more dangerous than the Germans. As Italians, this neo-Fascist Gestapo group found it easier to gather information in relation to the activities of the escape organisation and within a short space of time they had built up a network of informers. The additional manpower enabled Koch, working together with Kappler, to enhance their security crackdown. They had identified that a number of radio transmitters were operating in the city illegally. Their investigations led them to conclude that one of them was located in the Via delle Impero where the Chevaliers lived. One afternoon Paul Chevalier called to his mother's house and alerted her to the fact that there was a security sweep planned for the area that evening. The four soldiers who were hiding there, together with some of the younger daughters, went separately for walks through the city. Just before seven o'clock there was a discreet knock on the door and it was the porter, Egidio, alerting Mrs Chevalier to the fact that the raid was about to take place. The next knock was the raiding party of troopers. They searched each of the rooms and challenged Paul for his papers which were acceptable, being from the Swiss Legation. They questioned Mrs Chevalier as to the size of her family and she explained that herself, her five daughters and her mother lived there while her son lived at the Legation. Not for the first time, the size of her family and the limited accommodation available fooled a search party into thinking that nobody else could possibly be living there. There was a pile of gramophone records in one corner of the living room and one of the SS men began to search through them. Gemma, one of Mrs Chevalier's daughters, became very concerned as she remembered then that there was a British disc in among them. Luckily he did not notice it. After the search of the house and the entire area was over, Gemma went to collect her sisters and the soldiers who began to re-assemble in the room. By nine o'clock that evening they were all having supper. There were five British soldiers in the apartment for the next raid and this time it was the porter's wife, Elvira, who raised the alarm. Again the soldiers evacuated but, as it turned out, the objective of the raid was other apartments in the same block.

The increasing numbers which had been allocated to Kappler's group, together with the setting up of the separate group under Koch, enabled the authorities to gain tighter control on the city. One plain-clothes member of Koch's group was posted more or less permanently on the street where the Chevalier family lived. Cigarettes were invariably in high demand among the escaped soldiers. These were usually circulated by the priests but, on this particular occasion, some of the soldiers in the Chevalier apartment had none, so Gemma went to the local shop. As she handed over the money to make the payment, something in the face of the shopkeeper alerted her to danger. She left the shop and she noticed an Italian man watching her. So instead of walking towards the family home she went the other way and he began to follow. As the noise of his footsteps rang louder she decided to make a getaway and ran into the main street right across the path of an oncoming tram. Passers-by assumed she had been struck but when the tram passed through all that was left strewn on the street were large numbers of loose cigarettes. Gemma had got away. She kept this near miss from her mother for some time. These episodes were a portent of more serious developments to come as the new year dawned.

As Christmas approached, the pursuit of the Jews was stepped up. Again, Mother Mary records the developments:

> Unpleasant news this morning. The patriots and Jews who have been sheltered in religious houses all over Rome will probably not be safe any more. The Fascists – not the Germans this time – are raiding them. Back in October, when the SS men first got here, they tried to search the Oriental Institute, but desisted on learning it was pontifical property. The 'Republican Fascists' on the other hand, are quite free from such scruples and enjoyed breaking into anything belonging to the Pope because they are so very very sensitive at not having their Government recognised by the Vatican . . . their first venture was on a fairly large scale, including three neighbouring establishments. The Lombard College . . . the Oriental Institute run by the Jesuits and the Russicum, the College for Russian Church students . . . at the Oriental Institute, the Jesuits had sheltered three Jews. The Brother porter faced the Fascists and said 'you have no right here, this is Pontifical Property, where are your papers?' 'Here', was the answer, and the Brother found himself looking into the muzzle of a revolver. During the search one of the Jews escaped. The second was suffering from heart disease and collapsed from the shock of being discovered. The third was a doctor and although he could have escaped

quite easily he would not leave the man who had fainted. They were both taken.

Only three were caught in the Russicum but it was searched like the other two houses. As he was going, the leader of the gang turned to the Rector and said 'why did you hide these men' 'For the same reason for which we shall probably be hiding you before long' said the Rector.[15]

(*Mother Mary St Luke*, 22 December 1943)

In that period of November–December, the work of the organisation developed quite significantly. By Christmas they were catering for approximately 2,000 escapees, of whom about 80 were located in Rome.

The Monsignor was anxious that Christmas would be celebrated to the greatest possible extent. Simpson recalls visiting O'Flaherty's room on 23 December, which he describes as being:

. . . crammed with hundreds of small parcels, all wrapped in gaily coloured paper and tied with red silk ribbon. In the centre stood a middle-aged English lady, Miss Stanley, an enthusiastic aide to the Monsignor who had prepared all these Christmas gifts for the men in hiding . . . Squeezing in were priests – Maltese, Irish and New Zealand – mustered here to distribute these gifts throughout the city.[16]

Simpson and Furman were very busy on Christmas Eve. They distributed turkeys, wine, cigarettes and the special Christmas parcels prepared by Miss Stanley to all the billets.

On Christmas morning Mrs Chevalier served us brandy instead of tea. The house was a circus. Christmas gifts had already been exchanged among the family and the three British 'lodgers'. Even old Grandma was hobbling around happily. In the kitchen Rosie laboured over the Christmas dinner. On every sideboard and shelf in the dining room dishes groaned with cakes and fruit.[17]

St Stephen's Day in the Monsignor's room was one of great celebration, and as Derry describes it, there were visitors in and out in a never-ending procession. During the course of the day priests of half a dozen nationalities who were involved in the work of the organisation, diplomats and their families from the French, Polish, Yugoslav and other legations, Ambassador and Mrs Kiernan and their two daughters Blon and Orla, all turned up. A large number of unusual characters who were hiding in various parts of the College since well before Derry's arrival also joined the group. On more than one occasion, in his reports back to the authorities in Dublin, Kiernan refers to his wife using her singing skills to cheer up the members of the Irish community and others, and this was one such occasion when the group had a traditional sing-song. Aside from Delia, the main singer in this group was Fr 'Spike' Buckley. Indeed, his skill as a singer, while not matching hers, was so good that at various stages she tried to persuade him to have his voice professionally trained.

Indeed, visits to the Monsignor's room always had their less serious and sombre side. John Furman recalls:

> It was always in the nature of a treat to visit headquarters in the Monsignor's room. Quite apart from the tonic effect of a meeting with Sam, the Monsignor himself and John May, and the opportunity such a meeting presented of discussing our problems, there were invariably other visitors who were full of interest in their own right. Many were priests who gave more and more of their time to the work of their organisation as the number of prisoners drifting into Rome increased. Among them were Fathers 'Spike' Buckley and 'Edmund' Madden were most popular. They were a pair of crazy Irish men, game for anything. Spike, when mellowed with wine would sing sentimental Irish ballads to order.[18]

He also has clear memories of visits by the Irish Minister and his family to the Monsignor's apartment.

> The Irish Minister, Mr Kiernan, his wife and two daughters would occasionally put in an appearance. Mr Kiernan, a man of great erudition and an expert of fiscal matters, was soft-spoken and shy. His younger daughter, a very sweet seventeen was like him in manner, while Blon, the elder daughter, had the vivacious, quick alluring charm of her

beautiful mother. They were a musical family and when Mrs
Kiernan could be persuaded to sing, no greater tribute could
have been paid to her than the silence which immediately
descended over the Monsignor's habitually noisy room.[19]

As the year end approached, MacWhite reported on the
increasingly difficult security situation:

> After some weeks of tranquillity disturbances have again
> broken out in Rome. The shooting of two Fascist officials
> provoked reprisals and counter reprisals. Some Germans
> were also killed by hand grenades . . . since then, bomb
> explosions are more frequent and a few soldiers were killed
> in front of the German headquarters.[20]
>
> (MacWhite, 23 December 1943)

> A census of population has now been taken in Rome in order
> to force from their hiding places all those who are on the run
> of whom it is estimated there are one hundred thousand
> Italian soldiers, three thousand escaped prisoners of war and
> some hundreds of Jews. Only those whose names figure on
> the census paper will get food tickets. The concierge of each
> house must keep a list of the names of the occupants on each
> floor posted up at the entrance so that in case of a raid the
> supernumeraries may be seized. Nobody can change his or
> her residence without having first obtained permission from
> the police.
>
> The food situation is getting out of control. Due to
> cessation of rail transport and German requisitioning
> commodities no longer arrive. So far, there has been no
> distribution for the month of November of butter, sugar, rice
> etc . . . vegetables come from neighbourhood at present but
> as fighting approaches this source will dry up.[21]
>
> (MacWhite, 30 December 1943)

Meanwhile Ristic Cedomir submitted an end of year report to
O'Flaherty.

> In connection with the mission entrusted to me i.e.
> distribution of funds in supporting English and American

prisoners of war hidden in the valley of the river Arda . . . I am honoured in submitting to you the following statement asking for your kindness to hand it over to all interested persons.

He goes on to report on those who were being assisted to escape from the north of Italy to Switzerland.

The departure to SWITZERLAND is organised by groups under the direction of special guides – professional smugglers working for money . . . The spot from which they parted was PEDINE near MORFASSO, from the house of AUGERI GIANETTA who lived in ENGLAND for 7 years and has spent till now about 260,000 Lire from her private means in supporting prisoners.

The informal nature of the organisation is well illustrated later in that report:

In FLORENCE I left the sum of 1,000 Lire for two British Officers who were hidden together with Yugoslav Officers. I handed the money to the Serbian Orthodox Bishop INICI DORDOVIC former President of the English Club at SEBENIK, living now in FLORENCE.[22]

8

A Night At The Opera

The Lucidis were keen opera-goers and they, together with Simpson and Furman, went fairly regularly. Of all their visits to the opera, the initial one on New Year's Day 1944 was the most memorable. That first night of the new year in the Rome Opera House – one of the most beautiful in the world – was a very grand affair. The box that the Lucidis had booked was second to the left from the Royal Box in the centre. The Royal Box was empty because of course the King and his family were no longer living in the city. Simpson's description is interesting and conveys to some degree at least the unreal situation that pertained in Rome:

> The box between us and the Royal Box started filling up with high-ranking German Officers. Seated closest to them in the open curving front of our own box Adrienne too had seen them. In fact, from where she sat, she could have leaned over and touched the nearest German. With her profound hatred for the Nazis, she was finding it difficult to remain calm.
>
> John Furman, craning over to see what was going on, pointed. Down the centre aisle walked Captain 'Pip' Gardner and Lieutenant Colonel 'Tug' Wilson . . . In the left of the stalls, Rendell and Dukate . . . were waving to us. All around them sat German uniforms. To avoid the curious glances of the Germans in the next box, John and I moved back.[1]

On the programme that night was Puccini's *Tosca*. The cast was an outstanding one including Maria Caniglia, Beniamino Gigli and Tito Gobbi. At the interval, the boxes emptied as people moved for refreshments. Simpson noted that one of the German officers was clearly a high-ranking one. The programmes which had been issued to the audience were on rich parchment with gold embossed lettering and long silk cords. Simpson decided that he wanted to keep his as a souvenir. He also said to Renzo Lucidi that he would like to get an autograph, but the Italian was somewhat surprised when Simpson said the autograph he wanted was of the German General. So when the audience resumed their seats:

> Adrienne flashing a glamorous smile gave the programme to the General three feet away. Would he be so gallant as to autograph it, she asked in French. I watched the General's face light up with pleasure as, slightly embarrassed he took the hastily proffered pen off one of his aides and scrawled his long signature across the front of the programme.[7]

Simpson now had the autograph and signature of General Mackensen, Commander-in-Chief of the German Fourteenth Army. This could have been very valuable but as it happens it never proved to be necessary as the organisation's forgery efforts under the direction of Princess Nini were now so expert. Indeed, John May some time later got even better passes for them by taking advantage of the Vatican Secretariat.

The Vatican Secretariat, from time to time, submitted to the German Ministry requests for passes for officials of the Vatican who had to travel through Rome during the hours of the curfew. May managed to be in the right place at the right time in the office of the Secretariat when they were preparing a pile of passes for consideration by the German Ministry. Of course he had no business hanging around such an office but this was part of his talent, and while he was there, he secreted within the pile three in respect of Furman, Simpson and Pollak. The subterfuge worked to perfection. Passes for the three British officers on official documentation were made out and signed by the German Minister and returned to the Vatican Secretariat where May managed to be hanging around again and recovered them and passed them on to Derry. Accordingly, all three were now in possession of genuine – as distinct from forged – passes.

A number of the escapees became very fond of the opera and made regular visits, to such an extent that the Germans became aware of them. One night O'Flaherty was tipped off that the audience was going to be checked one by one for their papers. So two of the daughters of Mrs Chevalier found themselves attending a performance of *The Barber of Seville* in the Opera House on the tickets that had been secured for Furman and Simpson. They had never been able to attend before because of the price of the tickets.

Garrad-Cole meanwhile had been issued with false identity papers and began to move around Rome.

> There were plenty of German soldiers in the street. Most of them seemed to be sight-seeing and were probably on Christmas leave from the front in the south. They paid no regard to me when I stood alongside them admiring the beauties of Rome, and this encouraged me to get over the feeling of being a fugitive on the run . . . We used to foregather occasionally for lunch in a restaurant called 'The Bear' which stood in a narrow side-street close to the River Tiber. It was quite a fashionable establishment and the barman, Felix, had once worked in the Savoy Hotel in London. He knew us to be prisoners of war and kept our secret. If we walked into the bar when Germans were present, all we had to say was 'schnapps' and Felix would pour out a whiskey from a bottle under the counter. In most of the restaurants in Rome it was necessary to produce a ration coupon before it was possible to obtain a meal. The proprietors of 'The Bear' however, obtained most of their food from the black market and did not ask for coupons.[3]

Garrad-Cole found money to be a problem when he came to Rome originally but he had made contact with a person who was prepared to cash cheques made out on pieces of ordinary paper. These cheques were all presented to his bank in London and honoured without any question. He does not record the name of this person but it was almost certainly John May.

Early in the new year the Vatican authorities, having received a complaint, closed the gate which led from the street into the courtyard beside the Holy Office and then onto the German College. This meant that every visitor to O'Flaherty had to pass through the heavily guarded checkpoint at the Arco delle Campane. It also meant that O'Flaherty, in taking anyone from the German College into the Vatican, had to go the long way around and cross some Italian (as distinct from Vatican) property, so he was at risk of being captured. Aside from the guards, the disadvantage of this location was that it was far more public. This new arrangement was put in place without any prior notice shortly before Joe Pollak was due to call one day. Unaware of the change, he hammered so persistently and so loudly at the gate that eventually a Roman policeman walked up and demanded to know what he was doing. The best that Pollak could think of on the spot was to say 'nothing' and he walked away. Quite why the policeman did not suspect this, and question him further, is not clear. John Furman was due to arrive next but O'Flaherty was able to arrange for Fr Sneddon to go out and intercept him. He was able to show Furman a way through the Porto Santa Marta behind the colonnades on the left of St Peter's but this entrance meant he had to produce his Italian State identity card and inform the Swiss Guard whom he wished to see.

On 6 January Furman, Simpson and Pollak arrived together at the Porta Santa Marta, itself a most unusual step to take and very risky as the three were more likely to draw attention to themselves than if they arrived singly. As luck would have it, from his usual position at the top of the steps, O'Flaherty saw them coming and took them into the Guardroom which May had arranged could be used in those circumstances. Then, waiting for an opportunity when the coast was clear, he dispatched them one by one into the German College and up to his room where Derry was based. The situation, as it was explained to O'Flaherty and Derry, was extremely grave.

The previous evening, quite by chance, Furman and Renzo Lucidi had met in the street the French officer Henri Payonne who had come into Rome with Iride. He reported that a breach of security among escapees in the north of Italy around the Sulmona Camp had led to the arrest of eighteen Italians and there was a danger that information in relation to the work of O'Flaherty and his colleagues had leaked out either through bribery or torture of some of these Italians. As it was almost curfew time, Furman and Lucidi had to head back to the latter's apartment but they gave Payonne the telephone number. They warned him not to give it to Iride or anyone else because the security procedures that Derry had put in place required that as few people as possible knew of the activities of others. However, early the next morning a telephone call came and it was from Iride. She asked to speak to Pollak and she told him she must see him at once. While he was debating whether or not he should meet her, with Simpson, Furman and Lucidi, two further telephone calls came from her imploring him to come to her. When the telephone rang for the fourth time Lucidi's wife, Adrienne, answered it and it was from Payonne warning that everyone was in danger and they should clear out of the apartment at once. Simpson, Furman and Pollak immediately moved all their belongings into the rented apartment on the Via Chelini. They then rushed from there to meet O'Flaherty.

They debated the situation. Derry and O'Flaherty were of the view that the request to meet Iride was a trap whereas Pollak felt he should go because it was the only way to find out what was happening. Finally, at noon, he left to keep his meeting with her. The arrangement was that if the Monsignor had not heard from him by mid-afternoon, they could assume that he had fallen into a trap. At 4.00 p.m., a young Italian arrived with a note which was to be handed only to Patrick (the code name for Derry). This caused great alarm because they felt now it was another trap. Eventually they agreed that the best one to go down was Furman. Derry had very little Italian and it would be too risky to involve the Monsignor. When Furman went down he managed to persuade the young Italian to hand over the note. It confirmed that Iride had been captured, as had her mother, her sister and her own child. She had asked Pollak, using his codename Giuseppe, to come to see her because it was the only way to ensure the survival of her family. In the letter she stated:

> I won't talk unless threatened that I endanger the life of my
> baby by not doing so – in which case I shall poison myself. I

beg you, however, to save the lives of my baby and my poor mother. You must not believe that if they take Giuseppe that it is a betrayal – he is of no interest to them – they only want to know who supplies the money and I repeat that they will never know from me – I prefer death – I am only afraid Giuseppe may talk if he believes himself betrayed.[4]

When Pollak arrived at Iride's boarding house he immediately sensed that he was going into a dangerous situation and made a run for it. A chase through the city ensued, ending when Pollak attempted to enter a building. He spoke to the porter in Italian: 'I am an escaped British soldier. Please help me.' Since he was small and dark, very Italian-looking and dressed in civilian clothes, the porter thought he was a thief on the run from the police and replied in Italian 'and I am the Pope'. Pollak was captured. In the excitement of the phone call which Adrienne Lucidi received, she had forgotten that Payonne had mentioned that Pollak should not keep this appointment.

O'Flaherty and Derry realised this was a time of great danger for the organisation. While they were certain Pollak would never betray them, Iride's situation was particularly difficult bearing in mind that her entire family had been captured. Of all the various local helpers they had, she was one of those who knew most about the activities of Monsignor O'Flaherty and Major Derry. The fact that Iride and Pollak had been taken back to Sulmona the next day was reassuring to some extent. It almost certainly meant that the Germans were still investigating what was happening in that area and had not managed to obtain information about what was going on in Rome, either from Pollak or Iride. However, it was always possible that Iride would disclose information in the days ahead, so Derry made the decision to clear out the Via Chelini apartment.

The next blow to the organisation, ironically, was not aimed at it at all. One of the major preoccupations of the Gestapo at that time was to try and capture as many of the Italian Communists based in Rome as they could. During the morning of Saturday 8 January, two plain-clothes officers called on a widow whose Communist son was in the Regina Coeli prison. They introduced themselves as members of the Resistance and she of course did not realise they were actually from the Gestapo. They told her they had just been released from the prison and they had arranged a plan to assist with the escape of her son who was being constantly tortured. The plan was that her son would pretend to break down under questioning and offer to lead the Germans to the hideout of his Communist friends. His friends, however, would be ready and, in the ambush, the Germans would be killed and the prisoner, her son, would escape. Her part in this scheme was to get all her son's Communist friends together and arrange for the ambush. This she agreed to do, in her innocence. She took them along to meet Nabolante, who was a leader of the Italian Resistance, but also was one of those who regularly housed people for O'Flaherty. At that stage, he had living with him the two British army men, 'Tug' Wilson and 'Pip' Gardner whom Furman had waved to on the night of the opera. Within minutes, uniformed SS men arrived and arrested Nabolante, together with Wilson and Gardner. They left behind some Gestapo agents with Nabolante's cook, who was an old man and not difficult to frighten. This old man knew of the existence of the apartments in the Via Firenze and Via Chelini and indeed, even more dangerously, knew of the secret code via the doorbell which was used to gain admission. Furman in the meantime had arrived at the Via Chelini billet to arrange for it to be vacated in accordance with Derry's decision. Shortly afterwards, Nabolante's cook arrived with the two men who had originally deceived the widow. When they arrived, Furman answered the door and the cook told him that Gardner and Wilson had been arrested. It struck Furman as curious that two men were there also because obviously the cook could have delivered that message himself.

> I did not like the look of the cook's two companions. They did not strike me as individuals who would go out of the way to help anyone. I could not define my suspicions but I knew I did not like them. We entered the empty dining room and I said 'I can't understand why the cook brought you along with him. It was nice of you to keep him company but it seems so unnecessary . . . Before you go', I said, 'would you mind showing me your identity cards?' Everything that followed

happened in a flash. There was a roar of German voices in the passage outside and the two men pulled, not identity cards but revolvers from their pockets . . . a half dozen SS men, armed to the teeth, poured in.[5]

Arrested immediately were five officers, two privates, one American Air Force sergeant, Bruno Buchner the Yugoslav and Herta the Austrian girl who acted as housekeeper and, of course, Furman.

Herta was magnificent. Her prospects were far worse than ours. While we could at least hope to establish our identity as prisoners of war, she was an Austrian and, as such, would be regarded as a traitor by the Germans. She stood there calm and self-possessed.[6]

His first thought was how to get a message of warning to Derry and also how to keep Simpson away because the latter was due back at that apartment within the next few minutes. As all those who had been captured were lined up, he noticed that two soldiers who had been in the basement, Lance-Corporal Dale and Gunner Jones, had not been captured. He hoped that they had got away to convey the information to Derry. He also heard the doorbell stutter once or twice and then stop.

It sounded as though there might be a faulty connection. Another soldier asked my guard, 'did the bell ring then'? He replied, 'I thought so, but I am not sure'. One of the soldiers walked slowly to the door and opened it. Nobody was there. He tried the bell. It did not ring, lucky Bill, the failure of the bell had saved him. It was he who had rung before.[7]

It emerged subsequently that Bill Simpson had indeed rung the bell but while he was waiting for an answer the porter had signalled to him frantically from her room not to go upstairs. He was actually out of sight on the first floor landing when the flat door was opened and he saw the German soldier trying the bell. The two men who had been located in the basement had indeed managed to escape and made their way to the Swiss Legation to pass on the details of the ambush. They then left the Legation but were picked up again by a police check shortly afterwards. Meanwhile, an army Major called D'Arcy Mander, who was due to stay at the flat that night, returned and was also arrested. He, however, managed to make his escape and was never recaptured.

> It must have been about 3.30 p.m. on a fine afternoon in early January that I walked down the Via Chelini . . . waited for the coast to clear before going in . . . gave the signal on the bell. The door opened . . . Nobody was visible because nobody was there except for two figures in uniform in the hall, one of whom held a rifle pointed at my stomach and the other, who said in German: what do you want? I would like to say I put on an act and pretended to be frightened but let us say it wasn't very difficult![8]

Eventually the two soldiers decided that Mander would have to wait until the captain arrived to question him.

> The soldiers indicated a bench in an unfurnished front room which led from the hall through an archway and the shutters of which were, like the others, kept permanently closed as these windows gave onto Via D. Chelini and told me to wait there. They sat on a bench outside . . . I crept mouse-like to the window, slowly pulled the shutter strap and silently lifted the shutter a little. There, looking up at me from the pavement below was Cesare Coen, the fiancé of our nice Jewish girl who had lived in the basement part of the flat and who had cooked, washed and rendered for us there. I put my finger to my lips, enjoining silence, put my legs to the sill like a high jumper on the bar and dropped down to the pavement about ten–twelve feet below and ran. There was no pursuit, no shots, all was quiet. My absence had not been spotted, and I am sure, that when the Capitano arrived, the guards agreed to say that nobody had called at the flat rather than admit that anyone had got away.[9]

Mander went on to spend the remainder of his time in Rome as an undercover agent for the advancing forces. While he sought O'Flaherty's help from time to time for people he came across, he, like others, specifically avoided involving the Monsignor in any of the espionage in which he was engaged or in supporting it in any way, financially or otherwise.

Meanwhile Simpson hurried to get word back to the Monsignor.

> Half an hour later at St Peter's I ran all the way up to the now familiar room, where I found Sam and the Monsignor. 'Chelini's had it! and John along with it', I blurted out. Their faces fell. I filled in the sparse details I knew.[10]

This breach of security in the escape organisation caused great concern to Derry and O'Flaherty.

> 'Bruno and Herta'll get a rough time,' murmured Sam, almost to himself. 'If they make them talk.' 'Well, at least they don't know who Mrs M is, but Bruno knows about us here, Monsignor. They would give their eye teeth to know what is going on. If they feel they have got a case, there is nothing to stop them from raiding.' 'Just let 'em try it!' interrupted the Monsignor, with a grim expression. 'If any of these scoundrels ever dare to come near this room, I will beat the . . .'[11]

'His vehemence surprised me; but he was deadly serious,' Simpson recalled later. There was, of course, always the danger that the Germans would raid the Monsignor's accommodation. It was only extra-territorial, and so was not, strictly speaking, part of the Vatican. From the street outside there was no obstacle to anyone wishing to carry out a raid. He had always refused to keep firearms. He did, however, keep a coil of rope under his bed. In the event of a raid, his hope was that he would be able to escape through the window down into the courtyard.

On the way by lorry to the Regina Coeli prison, using a blanket on his lap as cover, Furman managed to tear his identity documents and his notebook with coded addresses and telephone numbers of the organisation into tiny fragments and pushed the bits, a few at a time, out of the lorry. In the prison, Furman learned that the cook had also led the Germans to the Via Firenze apartment where three South Africans were arrested.

It was now of the utmost importance to establish whether other locations had been raided or not. O'Flaherty sat down at his desk and, working the telephone for a number of hours, contacted every one of his priests and clerical students to warn them of the position and also asked them to check on the billets insofar as they could. In general, the billets were with private families and a visit from a priest would not be suspicious. Even if the billet had been detected by the Germans, a visiting priest would not necessarily be compromised. There was a worry that, if a large number of the billets were under observation, and they were all visited by priests during the course of one day, eventually the German intelligence work would point clearly to O'Flaherty. So all the priests were warned that they should not enter any billet unless they were reasonably sure it was not being watched. Those of O'Flaherty's helpers who had Vatican passes, which allowed them to bypass the curfew, worked through the night walking swiftly from home to home and being very careful to keep an eye out for SS or Koch's men. At dawn, more went into action. The most dangerous task was assigned to Fr Owen Sneddon, the New Zealander, as he had to check out the Via Firenze apartment which was felt to be the one most at risk. He approached it very slowly, taking good care to observe everything around him. As luck would have it, just as he reached the property, he managed to see the Italian porter whose face clearly conveyed to him that there was a problem and so he passed the apartment entrance and continued to walk down the street. The porter eventually caught up with him and explained that the Via Firenze apartment had been raided. In the succeeding hours and days however, it became clear that this was the limit of the breach of the organisation's security as all the priests reported back that the other locations were safe.

New security arrangements were immediately put in place by Derry. Escapees were moved to different billets and a strict limit was put on the amount of knowledge available to those who were assisting the groups. The total picture was known only to O'Flaherty, Simpson and Derry. Clearly, however, Kappler, Koch and their associates knew what was going on in general terms. Intimation of this came in the form of an invitation to O'Flaherty to attend a reception at the Hungarian Embassy. This particular Embassy was one that the Germans often chose for informal diplomatic activities. Accepting this invitation would involve O'Flaherty leaving the sanctuary of his accommodation and there was a suspicion it might be a trap, given recent developments. However, in typical fashion, he decided to attend. As it turned out, there were not many guests but the German Ambassador was one of them. Towards the end of the evening, von Weizsaecker asked the Monsignor for a quiet word. The Ambassador explained to the Monsignor that they knew precisely the activities he was involved in so, while the Ambassador would guarantee him safe conduct back to the Vatican that night, he added, 'If you ever step outside Vatican territory again, on whatever pretext, you will be arrested at once. Despite the consequences one could foresee, that decision has been agreed in your case and I cannot alter it. Now will you please think about what I have said?'[12]

O'Flaherty smiled down at the Ambassador and in a cheerful voice, which he raised so others in the room could hear, replied, 'Your Excellency is too considerate. I will certainly think about what you have said . . . sometimes.'[13]

At that time also O'Flaherty was summoned to a meeting with Monsignor Montini. This presumably arose as a result of a complaint from the German authorities and maybe critics of O'Flaherty's activities within the Vatican.

> Apart from the representations made by von Weizsacker, O'Flaherty's definite unpopularity with some of the Italians in the Vatican Civil Service made matters worse for him. Foreigners of any nationality have never been welcomed in the Vatican service and O'Flaherty's unique rise to office in the Urban College, his career in the Diplomatic Service and his appointment to the Holy Office had all been viewed with envious distaste by many Italians.[14]

As we have seen, the population of the Vatican is usually in the order of 500. It is reasonable to assume that, at this stage, everyone living in the Vatican had a fair degree of knowledge of what the Monsignor was doing. Certainly Montini knew, and obviously given the potential consequences if these activities became known, one can be certain he discussed this matter with the Pope, prior to meeting with O'Flaherty. We do not know the details of what transpired between Montini and the Monsignor but presumably the Irishman was instructed to curtail his activities. It seems fairly certain that if he were given a firm instruction to stop completely he would have followed it, out of a sense of loyalty to his Church. In any event if, having received such an instruction, he disobeyed it, there were many options open to the Vatican authorities to deal with the situation. It would have been a simple matter to transfer him either to the diocese in South Africa to which he was attached or indeed home to Ireland to take up other duties. Years later, the only clarification that O'Flaherty would offer was that 'I had my knuckles rapped pretty hard.'[15]

Derry noted that subsequently O'Flaherty greatly reduced his trips outside the Vatican, so it can be presumed that this was the directive he received from Montini.

Another development at that time related to Derry, who was still living in O'Flaherty's accommodation in the German College. The German Rector along with all the others in the College must have been aware for quite some time as to what exactly was going on. Presumably acting on complaints from the German authorities via the Vatican, he had decided he had to ask Derry to leave.

> The Monsignor entered the office, looking unfamiliarly grave. 'It is more trouble we are in,' he sighed. 'This time it's marching orders for you, me boy.' 'You mean I have to leave here?' 'Aye, that's about the size of it. Would you believe it now, the rector has just informed me that he has reason to believe that the gentleman who is a guest in my room is not a neutral Irishman at all, and he would be very much obliged if the gentleman would leave at once.'[16]

Both Derry and the Monsignor knew that the Rector, who was a German, was not a Nazi sympathiser so they concluded that he must have received some sort of warning from either the German or the Vatican authorities. Derry's immediate reaction was that he would have to seek accommodation in one of the billets used by escapees. However, at that stage it was quite clear that the Germans were well aware of Derry's activities as much as O'Flaherty's and so if he went anywhere in the city, it was only a matter of time before he would be picked up. The only alternative was to move him into D'Arcy Osborne's accommodation within the Vatican and so, donning the Monsignor's clerical garb once more, the British army Major moved, on 12 January 1944, to the accommodation in which he was to remain until the Allies took over Rome.

9

Warning Shots

Once he had settled into his new accommodation, Derry's first task was to see how those who had been captured were getting on. He asked D'Arcy Osborne to arrange for the Swiss diplomatic staff to visit the prison and see what could be done for Furman and the others, but this proved to be a bad idea. Many of the prisoners were held under false names and indeed in some cases the Germans did not even know who they were. However, if the Swiss went into the prison and visited these men, the Germans would immediately want to know how the Swiss were aware of their existence, which in turn would almost definitely lead back to the British Legation and O'Flaherty. This would have the effect of totally compromising the Vatican and creating huge difficulties. Of those who had been taken, the Germans particularly targeted the Yugoslav, Bruno Buchner, and some days later the Monsignor reported to his colleagues:

> 'We had sad news today, I had a note from Bruno. You remember we were worried about him after the raids on the flats? I have heard the Germans gave him a terrible time . . . he wrote me a note yesterday and somehow got it out. He said he was going to be shot this morning. He wanted me to know that he never opened his mouth once. Well, I got a message an hour ago. Bruno's dead. They shot him this morning.'[1]

Herta had been sentenced to five years' imprisonment and was sent back to Austria to serve it. At the end of the War, she was released and returned to Rome to settle there.

Aside from any commitment he may have given to Montini, clearly, from now on O'Flaherty had to be more cautious about his visits outside the Vatican. Apart from the danger of arrest to himself personally, any such event would almost certainly constitute grave embarrassment for the Vatican authorities. He had to rely more on the help of others than previously. With Furman and Pollak out of commission, a lot of the delivery work had been falling on Simpson. He reflected on what he had got himself involved in:

> So what if I had become part of this quasi-military but still amateur underground? After all, it had few rules, was led by a self-effacing, albeit magnetically strong Irish priest and Sam Derry, a Major, an energetic leader, and backed by the British Minister, but an escaper just like the rest and now involuntarily holed up in the Vatican. We were running by the seat of our pants. I was just an escaper, like the hundreds of others hidden across the city, like the five irrepressible American and British Officers in the French Seminary, the four British other ranks in Mrs M's where I was headed. After all, once you escaped, it was every man for himself, with a duty of trying to re-join Allied lines.[2]

Eventually, after debating this with himself, he realised his primary duty was to stay and help.

One of the groups O'Flaherty had contact with was the Greek underground movement. The leader of this movement, Evangelo Averoff, afterwards a Foreign Minister of Greece, visited O'Flaherty early in December with a colleague, Meletiou. They astounded O'Flaherty and Derry by telling them they had located a band of British escapees, about 120 miles from Rome and it was quite a distinguished group including a number of senior officers. Meletiou had departed with the instruction to bring back one of the officers which he did on 13 January, returning with Major General Gambier-Parry and Mrs Mary Boyd, an Englishwoman who had helped escapees in the Arezzo area. Gambier-Parry, who had been captured by the Germans in North Africa during 1942, but had managed to escaped, was at this stage the senior Allied officer on the run in Rome. The request was to get the General into the Vatican. This was a completely new situation for Derry because now he was dealing with an officer far senior in rank to himself so he felt he needed to discuss the situation with D'Arcy Osborne. Meanwhile he asked the Monsignor if he could arrange for a billet for Gambier-Parry and obviously they were seeking one of more than average security in order to ensure that the Germans did not capture him. In military terms, he would have been a valuable prize. The Monsignor had just such a place in mind in the home of a Signora Di Rienzo in Via Reggero Bonghi. She was English by birth. On the fourth floor of her accommodation, an end room had been walled up and from inside the house there was no indication that the room existed at all. The only entrance was through the window and even that was fairly precarious because it could only be reached when a plank was extended from another window. The plank linking the two rooms was approximately 40 feet above ground level. It was a perfect hiding place and the Major General was located there, nobody knowing where he was other than Derry, O'Flaherty and Br Pace who had guided him there. Subsequently the General had a note conveyed to Derry highlighting the suitability of the hiding place and the generosity of his hostess and her family. However, he expressed a desire to meet Derry as soon as he could, to try and assist with the work 'instead of sitting here in comfort and complete idleness'. Gambier-Parry was also anxious to discover more about the organisation and in particular, the chain of command and he asked Derry to clarify this for him.

> In fact, the General's letter brought home to me – I think, for the first time – the strangeness of this organisation, in which soldiers and priests, diplomats and communists, noblemen and humble working-folk, were all operating in concord with a single aim, yet without any clearly defined pyramid of authority.[3]

In his response, which was delivered by Br Robert, Derry described the arrangements as follows:

> Regarding 'chain of command', although I have tried to keep the show on military lines for the ex PW (on the whole

discipline has been good, although one or two of the boys have gone a little wild from time to time) we have no real chain of command between 'Golf' and his party and myself. We all work for the same end, I personally owe it all to 'Golf'. Consequently, 'Golf' sent me your letter to read and he will see your letter to me. He sends me daily an account of his activities and I keep him informed of everything I do.[4]

Eventually the General's frustration at his lack of involvement reached a level where he asked O'Flaherty for assistance and, without telling Derry, the Monsignor sent Br Robert to collect the General one evening. They took a tram to the Vatican where they met O'Flaherty and a group of his friends. As O'Flaherty, dressed in his full robes, brought the group across the Piazza to the Vatican and the papal apartments, he introduced the General, dressed in the best Donegal tweeds that could be found, to the saluting Swiss Guards: 'This is an Irish doctor friend of mine,' he said, 'He's been invited to His Holiness' reception also.'[5]

> The Monsignor led us around the rear of St Peter's. Climbing a long enclosed staircase, we emerged in the sunlight on a broad crowded balcony which overlooked the packed piazza some two hundred feet below . . . 'We are standing in the diplomatic enclosure', murmured the Monsignor, as he halted us in a clear space to the rear.[6]

Among those in attendance were members of the diplomatic corps including both the German Ambassador and the British Minister who had all been invited to the reception for the Pope's birthday. Without blinking an eye, O'Flaherty introduced Gambier-Parry as an Irish doctor to the German Ambassador and First Secretary Prince Bismarck who at all times made an effort to be friendly with everyone. The Prince invited 'the Doctor' to visit him sometime and Gambier-Parry replied with a promise that he would try. The Monsignor found it difficult to contain his amusement. Needless to say, Derry was appalled by this level of risk but he was not in a position to criticise the Monsignor because his senior officer, the General, had agreed to go along with it. As O'Flaherty remarked to Simpson, 'Sam'll be mad at me for this, bringing the General out of hiding, but I thought he should hear the Pope.'[7]

At the first opportunity he got, Derry took the Monsignor to task about this episode.

'Ah, the poor fellow needed a breath of air', he replied simply. 'He has been cooped up for weeks. Not good for him, you know.' 'Now look, Monsignor', I said earnestly, 'you know damn well I can't give him orders. He is a General, and if he chooses to go out and get himself recaptured, there isn't much I can do about it. But I have every reason for wanting you to stay in circulation, and, heaven knows, you have attracted quite enough attention already. I do beg you to be as cautious as you possibly can, at least until the German interest in you has died down a bit.' 'Never fear, me boy', said the Monsignor, treating me to one of his vast room-filling grins. 'Ah, a pity it is I haven't brought me clubs. We could have done a bit of putting practice. Nothing like golf for knocking all the troubles of this poor world out of your mind.' This was as far as we got. I sometimes suspected that Monsignor O'Flaherty's overriding interest in golf was his sort of secret weapon which enabled him to change the subject at will.[8]

Some time later, the General was moved to a hospital on San Stefano Rotundo run by the Little Sisters of Mary where he could exercise in the grounds and he stayed there until the Allies took over Rome.

By the middle of January, the number of escapees coming into Rome was reaching peak proportions and placing additional pressure on the organisation. Aside from prisoners of war who were the early clients of the organisation, there were now hundreds of civilians avoiding the authorities. These included former Italian soldiers or policemen and indeed others who had been called up for labour camps but had gone on the run.

In the meantime, the long-serving and heroic Mrs Chevalier had another narrow escape.

It was ten minutes before curfew one evening when Mrs Chevalier heard a knock on her door. When she answered there was a lame Italian youth outside whom she knew vaguely by sight. He warned her that the Germans were coming to raid after curfew time. He offered to bring her lodgers to a safe location. A quick decision then had to be made as to whether this was genuine or a trap. Her five lodgers at that stage, four British and one South African, were mindful of Derry's strict instruction that in the event of danger Mrs Chevalier had to be protected at all costs so they decided to go with the young Italian. Within ten minutes they were gone and the tiny apartment was set out to look as if it had just a family in occupation. Almost exactly on curfew hour, the Gestapo arrived and came in to carry out a search. They checked the papers of the Chevalier family which were all perfectly in order. Given the size of the accommodation the officer in charge was willing to accept that Mrs Chevalier was telling the truth when she claimed they were the only occupants. He made the assumption that the report of unusual movements into her apartment had been mischievous and asked had she noticed anything. The Maltese woman suspected that the information may have come from an apartment in a neighbouring block where well-known Fascist sympathisers lived. She directed the Germans to that location, advising that she had seen some strangers going in and out. For the next half hour, she and her family enjoyed the disturbance which emanated from the neighbouring apartment as a detailed and noisy search was carried out. When Simpson called the next day, he found that Mrs Chevalier wanted to have her lodgers back. As always, she was very difficult to dissuade, but Derry and O'Flaherty decided they would have to insist. Even though it was putting himself at considerable risk, O'Flaherty called the next day and insisted that her accommodation would have to remain empty of lodgers from now on. However, he agreed to transfer the five men to her friend Cecarelli, who was a butcher, and had been supplying meat to feed her lodgers since she got involved in the organisation.

A couple of nights later, there was a raid on the flat of Renzo and Adrienne Lucidi when everyone was in bed. Simpson and Fane-Hervey were living there, together with a Polish saboteur, Rafaelo, who had stored a bag of gelignite in the flat. In the time which it took for Renzo to open the door, the bag of explosives was hidden and Rafaelo was put into bed with Peppina the housemaid and told to pretend to be her lover. Simpson was told to act the part of the Lucidi's nephew. All of this worked to perfection, as it appears the Germans were concentrating on arresting Renzo Lucidi. It seems that they had found his name and details among others when searching the house of a Communist underground leader. In the rush, Fane-Hervey had not been alerted to this raid and did not know anything about it until a German arrived in his bedroom. Simpson's papers, provided by Monsignor O'Flaherty, which described him as a Milanese named Guglielmo Del Monte were examined and proved equal to requirements. In the confusion, the officers never asked Fane-Hervey for his papers. Immediately after the men left with Renzo, Simpson, Fane-Hervey and the Pole abandoned the accommodation. They had just gone a couple of hundred yards down the street when the Germans arrived back looking for them. The Lucidi's son, Gerald, concocted a story that Simpson and Fane-Hervey had come to play cards the previous night and were not really that well known to him or his family. The story about Simpson being a nephew seemed to have been forgotten by everyone, particularly the Germans, in the interim. However, on the second visit the raiders found an issue of a Communist Party newspaper in Gerald's room and they arrested him also. The boy was Adrienne's son by her former marriage and was French by birth so de Vial persuaded his Ambassador, Bérard, to intervene with the German authorities on behalf of the French embassy. This he did successfully and a few days later both were released.

The same night as the raid on the apartment, news came through to O'Flaherty of the arrest of Concetta Piazza who was a district nurse in a village north of Rome. She was the link between the Monsignor and approximately two dozen British prisoners of war who were hidden in various farms and villages around the area bringing them money and supplies. As luck would have it, she was at the end of a delivery run when she was arrested and so had no money or supplies on her that would be incriminating. She was taken to the Regina Coeli prison where she was charged with giving aid to Allied escapees.

On prison toilet paper she wrote a long letter to Field Marshal Kesselring setting out all she had done as a nurse to the benefit of all patients, including Germans, and protested that she was being prevented from continuing this work by her imprisonment. She persuaded a prisoner who was being released to smuggle her letter to O'Flaherty, who arranged for it to be typed up with a view to passing it on to the German commander. The question then arose as to how to get it to him. De Vial felt he could not go to Bérard again so soon after the previous case. An obvious choice, then, was Dr Kiernan in the Irish Legation. Because Kiernan had been seen to implement his country's neutrality policy to the letter, he would not have aroused suspicion among the German authorities. O'Flaherty used his friendship with Blon Kiernan to pass the letter on to her father and he in turn dispatched it, marked for the personal attention of Field Marshal Kesselring. Within two days the little nurse was released. Meanwhile, a new chief of police took up duty early in February.

> Pietro Caruso, another of the original fascists, dyed in the wool, one hundred per cent out and out . . . He is full of zeal in his new office and burning to show the republic what he can do in support of it.[9]
>
> (*Mother Mary St Luke*, 2 February 1943)

Caruso and Koch began to plan a major initiative. On the night of 3 February, an ex-monk who was part of Koch's group began to knock on the doors of St Paul's Outside-the-Walls crying for help. When the door was opened, Caruso and his men immediately swarmed into the building. The place was looted. Sixty-six people in hiding in the accommodation were arrested, many disguised as priests. They included a general, nine officers and other soldiers of the Italian army, former policemen and nine Jews. The Vatican made a strong and clear public protest at this incursion onto their property. The German authorities in the shape of the Ambassador denied any involvement. When the integrity of the Vatican was threatened, invariably the Irish Government lodged a protest. Kiernan was happy to be able to report back on 7 February 1944 to the Dublin Government that Cardinal Maglione had accepted these assurances and was satisfied that the intrusion was the work of Fascists. This whole episode was embarrassing from the point of view of the German authorities. At the same time, there was of course great concern in the Vatican that it might be the first of many such raids. Altogether at that stage 55 monasteries, 100 convents and other Vatican properties were hiding Jews. One of the leading authorities on the situation of the Jews in Rome is a survivor of the October 1943 raid, Michael Tagliacozzo. He estimates that 477 Roman Jews were sheltered in the Vatican while another 4,238 found refuge in the monasteries and convents in Rome. Some were employed in the Vatican Library and museums. Others were protected by being enrolled in the Palatine Guard. This is an honorary institution of guards and membership automatically confers Vatican citizenship. As Jewish people came under pressure, many were enrolled in the Guard and its membership increased from 300 in 1942 to over 4,000 by the end of 1943.

During autumn 1943 and early 1944, fierce fighting was under way between the Allied and German forces in the south of Italy. Indeed there was ongoing debate at military and political level among the Allies as to whether trying to secure the capture of Rome was a viable proposition and should be receiving significant priority. There was certainly a view among the US authorities that all spare resources should be directed towards the upcoming Operation Overlord which was the cross-channel invasion of France. Roosevelt was ready to accept this view and indeed Stalin repeatedly called on the Allies to take pressure off his army by bringing forward the date for the invasion of France. Churchill, meanwhile, was arguing for a continuance of the policy which had the capture of Rome as a high priority. The three had met in Tehran during late November and while the capture of Rome remained on the lists of objectives, it very much now took second place to the invasion of France in the allocation of any spare resources. Meanwhile, the American Fifth Army, under General Mark Clark, had continued to make painstakingly slow progress towards Rome in November and December. It was then decided to make an

Colin Lesslie, disguised as a monsignor.

Lieutenant John Furman.

L–r: *John Furman, Sam Derry, Henry 'Barney' Byrnes and Bill Simpson, 1946.*

German paratroopers on patrol at the limit of St Peter's Square.

Pietro Koch, Chief of the
Fascist Political Police Squad.

Civilians are dragged from their homes in the Via Rasella and lined up as suspects by the gates of the Barberini Palace.

Lieutenant Colonel Herbert Kappler, Head of the Gestapo in Rome. Photo taken in 1948 while he was on the way to his trial.

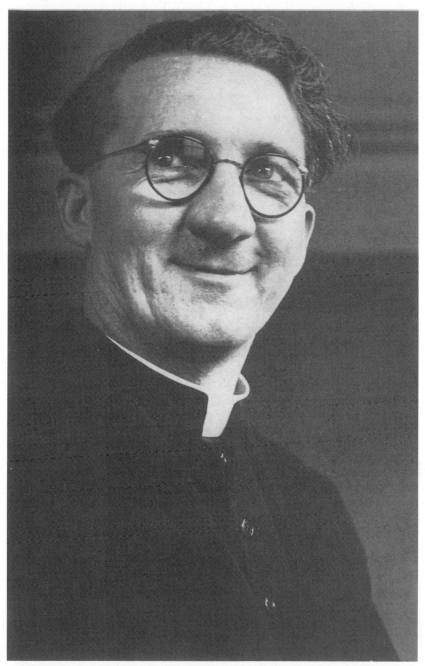

Hugh of 'the twinkling eyes'. Monsignor O'Flaherty in the 1950s.

Monsignor Hugh O'Flaherty receiving his honour from the senior American officer in Italy at that time, General J. C. H. Lee.

The Monsignor with Bill Simpson in the 1950s.

This is Your Life *19 February 1963*. *Hugh O'Flaherty (second from right, front row) and Sam Derry (fifth from left, front row) head and shoulders above the crowd. On the right of the photo, beside O'Flaherty, is the Cameron Highlander, Norman Anderson (wearing a kilt). To the left of Derry in the foreground are his sons Andrew, James, Richard and William; seated are Derry's wife, Nancy and their daughter, Fleur Louise. Everyone else is either a member of the rescue operation or an escapee.*

L–r: *Hugh O'Flaherty, Sam Derry and Eamonn Andrews, after the* BBC's This is Your Life *programme on 19 February 1963.*

The grave of Monsignor Hugh O'Flaherty, Daniel O'Connell Memorial Church, Cahersiveen.

amphibious attack on Anzio which was north of the defensive line that the Germans had taken up. The hope was that this attack would sever their supply lines and force them into a rapid retreat. The American forces landed on the Anzio beaches on 22 January and met little or no initial resistance.

This created great hope among the Allies then resident in Rome, and those favourable to their cause, as Anzio was approximately 30 miles south of Rome.

> During the night the Allies made a landing at Anzio . . . it seems too good to be true . . . people in the streets look happier than they have for a long time.[10]
>
> (*Mother Mary St Luke*, 21 January 1944)

The Duchess of Sermoneta reflected the general mood in her record of events:

> And then at last! After so much weary waiting . . . came the news that the British had landed in Anzio. Hope, ever flying with swift wings far ahead of events, convinced me and many others that the liberation of Rome was only a question of a few days.[11]

Within a week or so she was arrested herself and placed in detention. In fact, 50,000 men and 5,000 vehicles had landed, completely surprising the Germans. General Westphal, Kesselring's Chief of Staff, recorded:

> At the moment of the landing south of Rome, apart from certain coastal batteries there were only two battalions. There was nothing else in the neighbourhood which could be thrown against the enemy on that same day. The road to Rome was open. No one could have stopped a bold advanced-guard entering the Holy City. The breathtaking situation continued for the first two days after the landing.[12]

MacWhite was one of the many who were mystified,

> It appears that they encountered no opposition on their way. Why the Allies did not push forward at once . . . is a mystery which only the Allied High Command can explain . . . here

was one of the opportunities which Napoleon would have not have missed.[13]

(MacWhite, 26 January 1944)

Unfortunately, the Allied Commander did not take advantage of this opportunity and the initial optimism was dashed as the German forces managed to re-group and counter-attack, effectively containing the threat, and a stalemate situation developed which lasted for months.

> Despite the surprise landing and eight days without encountering any serious resistance the Allied situation on the bridgehead has deteriorated and important ground has been lost. They failed to exploit initial advantage and gave adversary plenty of time to bring up reinforcements . . . Failing the unforeseen it may well take months before the Allies reach Rome . . . The skirmishing between the Germans and the Vatican has taken a turn for the worst since the violation of the Basilica of St Paul. Italian newspapers which are under German control are bitterly attacking the Vatican for sheltering Jews and renegades from which colleagues conclude that a more serious violation of Vatican neutrality is not to be excluded.[14]

(MacWhite, 11 February 1944)

Churchill had hoped for more success as he was the main proponent of this strategy. 'I had hoped that we were hurling a wild cat on the shore, but all we got was a stranded whale.'[15]

Of course, among the Allied leadership, Churchill was the architect of the Italian strategy, whereas Roosevelt and Stalin favoured invasions of western or southern France. So the British Prime Minister was making sure that the blame for the relative failure at Anzio was not going to be laid at his door. He was successful in this with the result that the senior officer on the ground, the American Major General John Lucas, took the brunt of the criticism. More recent considerations of these events, however, have suggested that maybe Lucas was not provided with sufficient resources to reach Rome successfully. Alternatively, others have suggested that he was the wrong man for this sort of a job and maybe somebody of a more adventurous nature should have been appointed. Certainly, consideration was given to moving General George Patton to take charge at Anzio at one stage. Wherever the fault lies, certainly the landing at Anzio raised expectations among those in Rome that the Eternal City would be liberated shortly. However, there was growing concern in Rome and in Vatican circles that the city itself could become a battlefield.

Derry found himself having to discipline some of the Allied prisoners-of-war from time to time, usually because they were placing themselves or others in danger because of overindulgence in alcohol. A British Serviceman received the following letter:

> I have heard of the affair of a few nights ago when you were in an intoxicated condition. I really wonder if you can realise what is being done for you by various people (ie the people in whose house you live and the padre friends). Do you understand that as a result of an affair like that one of the other evening these people might have lost their lives and if anything like that had happened, you and you alone would have been responsible. It would have been a thing that would have been on your conscience all your life. From an official point of view I can assure you that such behaviour will not be tolerated. Any future conduct contrary to good order on military or naval discipline will have serious consequences afterwards.[16]

10

Chasing the Pimpernel

On the very day that Italy entered the war, Cardinal Maglione had begun negotiations with D'Arcy Osborne to ensure that Rome would not be bombed. While the British authorities could see good reasons for not bombing the Vatican they were unwilling to give an undertaking not to bomb Rome, particularly if Italian aircraft were to become involved in bombing British cities. This argument went to and fro for the next three years. The international laws that govern warfare recognise that there is the possibility for a city to be declared open. Under these circumstances, one of the warring parties undertakes not to use the city for military purposes. The opposing party then would accept that it had no reason to bomb the city, and the lives of innocent civilians and indeed, particularly in Rome's case, the treasures of history would be safe. The Vatican began to explore whether it was possible to apply such an arrangement to Rome. In the meantime, the Allied Forces invaded Sicily in July 1943 and parts of Rome were bombed in that attack leading to the loss of approximately 1,500 lives. This led to wide-scale expressions of concern from the governments of Catholic countries and diplomatic pressure began to increase on the US and UK Governments. President Roosevelt, in a broadcast on 23 July 1943, claimed that Rome was being bombed to save the lives of Allied soldiers fighting in Sicily and it was not possible to reach an open city agreement because the Axis forces were not willing. The Allied landing at Anzio brought the warfare even closer to the city. The papal palace at Castelgandolfo south of the city was bombed. Hundreds who had taken refuge there were killed. At the same time, battle was raging around Cassino and, as Christmas approached, shells were beginning to drop on the monastery of St Benedict there. The Vatican protested to both D'Arcy Osborne and Tittmann. The senior Allied officer on the front line in February 1944 was a New Zealander, General Freyberg. There was a debate among the various officers as to whether destroying the monastery was warranted and indeed there were rumours that it housed many refugees. In the event, Freyburg sought permission to bomb the monastery and this was granted. Meanwhile, the German Ambassador, von Weizsaecker, was assuring the Vatican that there were no artillery, mortars, machine guns or troops in the monastery or its immediate surroundings so there was no justification for bombing. Allied aircraft dropped leaflets warning of the impending bombing and the abbot requested everyone to leave but, before the evacuation was complete, the bombing commenced and approximately 100 refugees were killed. A propaganda war ensued. While a number of months elapsed before the Allies eventually captured Cassino, the bombing of the monastery caused great concern in Rome, particularly in Vatican circles. It seemed to them that no property was now safe from the effects of war. When the abbot of the monastery arrived in Rome and confirmed the truth of the German claim that the monastery had been unoccupied by any military personnel or equipment, these anxieties increased.

The fact that the front lines were now so much nearer Rome created additional problems for the escape organisation. Derry was concerned that some of those in hiding might act prematurely and get themselves recaptured. In the circumstances, with the pressure coming on the Germans, if anyone was recaptured they were almost certainly going to be shot immediately. The instruction was issued to all, via Simpson, that they were to stay in their current locations. Even the prisoners in Regina Coeli were becoming aware of the possibility of liberation. Furman, who was still imprisoned there, had managed to get a note out to Derry via an Italian barber who went into the prison most days. The note outlined how Furman had been captured and advised Derry of the names of all those British prisoners who were in captivity there. However, a second note came from him on 26 January reporting that all the British prisoners, including himself, were to be taken from the jail to an unknown destination. The prospects for Furman were extremely bleak and he acknowledged this in his note. He realised there was a good possibility he was going to his death. He wrote to Sam Derry:

> I have just had notice that all British prisoners are leaving here within the next two or three hours. It is the most damnable luck – to have 'missed the bus' by just over two weeks, but who knows, perhaps I shall see you in Rome yet. In any event, if I fail to make it, I know you will see my wife and Diana when you get back. Would you also ask Bill to remember me to all our friends who have been so kind to me. And would you greet our Irish golfing friend for me . . . I will sign off now with the hope that you have an uneventful voyage back to England and the work you have done here is duly rewarded.[1]

On 10 February, the Roman newspapers carried pictures of approximately 300 American prisoners of war being marched through the city by the German authorities. Such treatment of prisoners of war was of course completely contrary to the Geneva Convention but the Germans had been unable to resist what they saw as a very clever propaganda stunt.

Fr Ambrose Roche, an Irish Augustinian student from Clara in Offaly, was on the street as the prisoners were marched through. One of them asked for a cigarette so Fr Roche threw him the packet. He was immediately arrested by the Italian Fascist police and, although the Germans were willing to let him go, they insisted that he be imprisoned in Regina Coeli. By this stage, many of the Irish priests knew the Kiernan family well. Shortly after they arrived in Rome, the Minister and his wife had established an arrangement whereby the Legation operated an open house for Irish residents in Rome every Thursday afternoon. Fr Twomey recalls, 'Tea, coffee, biscuits and sandwiches were served, and there was whiskey, wine, brandy, sherry, whatever you wanted.'[2] When he heard about the young student's arrest, Kiernan began to act.

I had found it difficult to get into Regina Coeli, to interview the priest, although I was well provided with cigarettes to ease my entry. The policeman on duty, to my complaint, that it was a hard place to get into, dryly remarked that it was harder to get out of.[3]

The Irish Minister then used his valuable contacts in the German Embassy to secure the release of Fr Roche. The authorities did not realise that the young Irishman was very actively involved in O'Flaherty's organisation.

The prisoners were temporarily held in an old camp on the east of the city. On 12 February, Lucidi and Simpson got an urgent message to meet Monsignor O'Flaherty at his usual location outside St Peter's Basilica at eleven o'clock. When they met him, he explained that he had been contacted by an Italian family. They had taken in six Americans who had escaped from a detention camp and were now located in a farm house about two miles from the camp. The following day, Lucidi brought three of them to Mrs Chevalier's apartment followed at a twenty-minute interval by Simpson who brought the other three. By the next day, they had dispersed them through the city in safe accommodation. In the meantime, John Furman in company with Lieutenant J. S. (Johnny) Johnstone had managed to arrive back in Rome. It seems their escape was a carbon copy of Derry's own as they managed to jump from a train taking them north. Then Furman and Johnstone, with the help of some locals, managed to acquire bicycles and make good their escape cycling all the way down to Rome. In fact they were only a couple of miles from the Swiss border and safety, but they decided to cycle the four hundred or so miles to Rome to help the organisation in its work. Furman recalls their arrival in Rome:

I felt happy and suddenly relaxed as I watched Johnny's enchanted eyes taking in the beauty of the square, the colonnade, the obelisk, the fountains, the Swiss Guards and the Basilica itself. Rather self-consciously, we shook hands.[4]

Furman, with the help of a friendly priest, managed to send a note up to Monsignor O'Flaherty's apartment saying he was outside:

There was a look of incredulity on Monsignor O'Flaherty's face as he came bounding through the Santa Marta gate in response to the note I had sent up by the hand of a friendly monk. So soon as his eyes lit on me, he let out a roar and charged with cassock flying to where I was standing. Never was there such back slapping and hugging; security went momentarily overboard. Then holding me at arms length, he said in his rich Irish brogue, 'In the name of God, it is good to see you back, John. You are paler and thinner but you are all in one piece. This is surely a happy day for us all.'[5]

The Monsignor brought them down to the house where Frs Claffey and Treacy lived. Early in the afternoon, he returned bringing one of his own suits for Johnny who was about the same size as himself. They were able to go out and subsequently met up with Bill Simpson and Renzo Lucidi. Both moved in to live with the Pestalozzas. Before he left, Furman gave a note to the Monsignor for Sam Derry whom he was anxious to meet up with again: 'Back in Rome. Where the hell are you? One consolation for my sore arse will be when I see your smiling face.'[6] The effect of the long journey on their anatomies was clear in the cryptic comment. Derry was most anxious to link up with Furman. At the same time, he had to be very careful because one false move could have threatened the existence of the entire organisation and left the British Minister and the Vatican authorities in serious difficulties so he had to restrain himself. Furman went back to work with Simpson and almost immediately his alertness saved some lives. One day he received a tip-off that an Italian who had guided four escapees into Rome had been arrested and had begun to talk. This man knew nothing about the organisation, but he did know where the four escapees whom he had escorted to Rome were billeted. Furman managed to move them before the inevitable raid and put them into Mrs Chevalier's. This established a pattern for the future use of that accommodation as another clearing house available in an emergency.

From the beginning of her involvement, Mrs Chevalier tended to stay at home running her billet. Her daughters did all the necessary shopping for the household and bringing of messages to and fro. The exception to this was when she was called upon to provide medical assistance to the escapees in the various other billets around Rome. Her partner in this was Milko Scofic, a Yugoslavian who was studying medicine in Rome when the Germans first came into Italy. He was arrested at that time, sent to a slave labour camp in Serbia but this was subsequently overrun by partisans. He managed to make his way back to Rome having secured forged papers which allowed him to rejoin the university. He and the Maltese widow, who had some nursing experience, provided the main medical services to the escapees until later in the War. By that stage, among the group were a Scottish doctor, Captain MacAulay, and a South African dentist, Captain Kane-Berman, who were in a position to lend their knowledge and experience. Scofic subsequently qualified and had a distinguished medical career. His girlfriend (later wife) was a young Italian art student who later became famous as a film star: Gina Lollobrigida was a supporter of the Italian Resistance and indeed had assisted O'Flaherty's organisation from time to time. After her film career was over, she returned to her first love, sculpture.

From time to time, however, a case came to the attention of the organisation that they were unable to deal with, due to the lack of proper medical equipment. One of these was a Cameron Highlander, Private Norman Anderson, who had acute appendicitis. He was hiding on a farm near Subiaco, 40 miles northeast of Rome. Br Pace, who was his link man, made arrangements to have him deposited at a suitable hospital where he would undoubtedly lose his freedom but secure the necessary medical attention. However, Anderson was unwilling. Death was a preferable option, in his view. As so often in these difficult cases, O'Flaherty had a solution. The Irish authorities back in Dublin, had they known what their countryman was doing, would have been horrified. O'Flaherty contacted an old friend of his, Professor Urbani, who was a surgeon in one of the big Roman hospitals, which was now crammed with German patients who were there as a result of the fighting at Anzio. The Professor agreed to carry out the operation on O'Flaherty's friend. However, the patient had to be brought straight in, operated on and removed from the hospital immediately, to avoid giving rise to any awkward questions. Next, the Monsignor contacted Fr 'Spike' Buckley, his fellow countryman who had the same level of commitment and courage as himself. More importantly, Fr Buckley was built along the same lines as the Monsignor and his exceptional strength was going to be necessary in this escapade. Finally, the Monsignor made contact with his friend Delia Murphy. The real difficulty was getting Anderson to and from the hospital. An ambulance was out of the question, taxis were more or less non-existent at this stage and the few private cars available were in the hands of Fascists who could secure the necessary permits. The Ambassador's wife immediately arranged for Fr Buckley to drive the Legation car. She and Fr Buckley collected Anderson and brought him to the hospital. There he was handed over to the care of two nurses who were in the confidence of the surgeon. Within an hour he was collected again by Fr Buckley and brought in the Legation car, protected by the diplomatic plates, to Mrs Chevalier's apartment. On the way, they had a narrow escape. When they were stopped at traffic lights, they were approached by the SS. Fr Buckley explained that the man in the back was an Irish priest who was being taken to hospital. The patient looked so bad that this story was convincing enough and they were allowed to drive on. Fr Borg had already alerted Mrs Chevalier to this arrival and Milko Scofic was there to lend medical assistance. Anderson stayed there for approximately one week, during which time his medical condition was grave, until the lame Italian boy turned up once more and warned Mrs Chevalier that a raid would be carried out on her apartment in about two hours. At that stage she was catering for five fit escapees and they managed to disperse through the city. Anderson was in no condition to join them. Again Delia Murphy (Mrs Kiernan) was called upon and the Embassy car was used to move him to the safest location of all, which was the American College, where he was placed under the care of Colin Lesslie who nursed him back to health. In many ways this episode sums up the peculiar nature of the rescue organisation. As Derry sees it:

> Rarely has a man owed his life to such strangely assorted
> factors as a scholarly Monsignor, with the incisive brain of a
> business tycoon; a giant priest, with the strength of a lion and

the gentleness of a lamb; an Irish lady, whose humanity overwhelmed political propriety; a little Maltese widow, with a gallant heart as big as her own expansive family; and an Italian surgeon who, with his enemies all around him, risked his life to save a life.[7]

On another occasion, O'Flaherty did a solo run in relation to a medical emergency. An Austrian who was hiding in the accommodation of the Propaganda College came down with appendicitis. This time the Monsignor borrowed a car from a high Vatican official, and drove to the Propaganda College where he collected the Austrian, and took him to a hospital. Here the nuns who were in league with O'Flaherty put the man into a ward full of German officers and in turn prepared him for an operation which was carried out by a German military surgeon who had not an idea as to the identity of his patient. The nuns cared for the Austrian for a few days and then O'Flaherty took him back to the Propaganda College. All of this was done without any regard to his own safety.

Contacts in another of the Roman hospitals enabled O'Flaherty to come to the assistance of Tom Carini, who was one of the leaders of the Italian Resistance. Carini was in the Santo Spirito Hospital as a result of a genuine illness and also suffering as a result of torture by Koch. Two armed guards were allocated to ensure that he did not escape from the hospital and they took turns in position beside his bedside. It had been made clear to him that if he made any effort to escape he would be executed. However, his mother had made contact with the nuns and the Mother Superior had decided to assist with the freeing of Carini if at all possible. The nuns had noted that at approximately 2.00 a.m. each night the guard on duty was liable to go to sleep. At about that time one night, Carini was woken by the sensation of his feet being tickled and he was quite surprised to see it was the Mother Superior. She managed to move him from the bed, without disturbing the guard sitting nearby, and relocate him in the nun's dormitory where he stayed for the rest of the night. From what seems to have been a fairly endless supply, O'Flaherty had left a Monsignor's clothing with the Mother Superior. Carini donned this and sat with her saying the rosary until the early hours of the morning when O'Flaherty arrived and the two, dressed as Monsignors, walked out of the hospital.

March 1944 was a very difficult time for the organisation. The winter had been extremely harsh, increasing the numbers of those coming to Rome from the outlying areas seeking assistance. While Derry and his colleagues did their best to resource them and send them back into the outlying areas, the numbers continued to grow. Those coming in outnumbered those being relocated in the country areas. In the previous month, the numbers of escapees being catered for by the organisation within the city had risen from 84 to 116. Finding billets for them was terribly difficult and it kept all the senior members of the organisation stretched.

One of the trickiest cases they had to deal with was that of Paul Freyberg, a young Lieutenant in the Grenadier Guards, the son of General Freyberg. Paul had been captured near Anzio on the night of 7 February but had managed to make his escape two nights later and went into hiding with some Italian refugees who were sheltering from the Allied bombings. One of these was an elderly Italian who had lived for quite a while in America and so spoke English fluently. Freyberg found it impossible to penetrate German lines to reach his colleagues so this elderly Italian gave him civilian clothes and advised him to make for Castelgandolfo, which was only a few miles from where they were in hiding. He reached his destination some days later. Seeing the proclamation on the wall of the estate that this was papal property, he claimed sanctuary and was admitted. For the German authorities, his recapture would have been a great propaganda coup whereas for their counterparts in the Vatican, his presence on papal property was a potential source of embarrassment, if it became known. So, while some at least in the Vatican may have disapproved of O'Flaherty's activities, on this occasion they sought his assistance. The difficulty was that the Germans were located in strength between Castelgandolfo and Rome. An official Vatican truck made routine calls to the papal villa with supplies for staff and usually was allowed through unhindered because the personnel at the German checkpoint were very familiar with the routine. O'Flaherty organised for Freyberg to be taken the eighteen miles to Rome in the boot of the truck on its return journey and was brought safely into the Vatican.

> When the time came to leave I found that a small cavity had been made in the centre of the vehicle which was otherwise piled high with sacks of potatoes and crates of garden produce, and this niche was further hidden by being lined with thick sacking. There was a heartstopping moment when we reached the German road block on the outskirts of Rome and the doors at the back of the vehicle were thrown open but the search was perfunctory, and soon we were on our way again.[8]

As it happened, Freyberg was about to celebrate his twenty-first birthday and so a little party was arranged, to be held in the British Legation. A surprise visitor, much to Derry's delight, was John Furman whom he had not met since his escape from captivity. Furman had called into the German College and there had met Princess Nini, the first of O'Flaherty's unofficial guests, and the person who spent her time arranging for false papers.

> Nini told me she was going, with a party of people from the German college, to the little chapel which housed the British Legation. My ears pricked up at once and I asked whether I might join the party. She agreed, saying that as there would be seven or eight going, most of whom would be known to the guards on the building, it was unlikely that they would be stopped.[9]

Some time later another voice from the past made contact. Renzo Lucidi answered his phone and was surprised to hear the voice of Joe Pollak. Pollak said he was at the Via Chelini flat. This was a bit of a shock because the flat and the one at Via Firenze had been abandoned and there was a belief within the organisation that the person who had rented the flat on behalf of Monsignor O'Flaherty, a Dr Cipolla, was actually a double agent working for the Germans. In fact, Pollak had achieved a miraculous escape. He was taken to Sulmona, as the group had learned, and there was charged with being a traitor and a spy. However, he managed to recognise a German officer who was in a position to testify that he was in fact a prisoner of war and so his sentence was reduced to that of imprisonment in the camp. Pollak was to be moved to Germany. At the very moment they were being loaded onto a train to go to Germany, the RAF bombed the station at Aquila and in the confusion he was able to escape. Using his excellent Italian, he managed to secure a lift in a lorry heading for Rome. They were stopped at a checkpoint but Pollak managed to slip over the side of the lorry as it halted and he crawled underneath. The driver and Pollak's companion were arrested and the lorry was taken to the nearest German barracks with Pollak clinging to the underside. Just as it reached the barracks it had to slow down at a sharp turn, where he dropped off unnoticed and walked into Rome. As he was not up to date with recent developments, it was an obvious move for him to go to the Via Chelini flat. As it happens, his appearance was a fortunate development for Dr Cipolla because the doctor was looking for a means to get back on good terms with the escape organisation. The arrival of Joe Pollak afforded him the opportunity to do just that. He was treated with suspicion thereafter but did not betray any member of the organisation.

Of course, daily life in Rome was not without its lighter moments:

> Yesterday as a German Red Cross closed car was passing through . . . the doors at the back burst open as it hit a rough spot and two young pigs fell out. Unaware of his loss, the chauffeur continued on his road at a high speed. The pigs were collected by women from the neighbouring houses who rushed to the scene and a passing butcher volunteered his services.[10]

(*MacWhite*, 27 February 1944)

By the middle of March 1944, the organisation was huge. The total number of escapees and evaders whom they were looking after had increased to 3,423 and the number of accommodations in use in Rome was approximately 200. The organisation was spending three million lire a month (then the equivalent of about £10,000 or, in current terms, over €400,000). Among those being provided for in the countryside around Rome were approximately 400

Russian escapees who were being looked after by Monsignor O'Flaherty through a Russian priest, Fr Bezchctnoff, assisted by two Russian women who had formerly served in the Red Cross.

Occasionally, the position eased somewhat as the organisation was able to assist some hundreds of escapees to make their way out of Italy. At the same time, new cases were coming to their attention and as the numbers increased the financial burden also grew. Also growing was the frustration of the German and Fascist authorities. As we have seen, O'Flaherty understated the risk to himself on all occasions and we can never be sure how many near misses he had. As Lieutenant William Newnan of the United States army describes it:

> He was the good angel of all escaped prisoners until things got too hot for him and he had to retire into the Vatican. I cannot give you the details, but this worthy man risked his life for all of us day after day.[11]

The Monsignor was a long time personal friend of Éamon de Valera. Indeed when de Valera made his first visit to Rome as Taoiseach, it was O'Flaherty who looked after him and showed him around. Long after the War, the family made a visit to de Valera, who by then was President, in Áras an Uachtaráin. The Monsignor's nephew recalls him telling the President the details of one episode which he used to illustrate the way some German officers interpreted their instructions literally. It seems an officer and a number of German soldiers were sent with an instruction to arrest the Monsignor in a particular house in Rome. However, the Monsignor left a couple of minutes before they arrived and he actually passed them on the street. He was quite satisfied that they recognised him but the officer, interpreting his instructions exactly, took no action.

We know, however, that Kappler made at least three very organised and determined efforts to capture the Irishman over a period of months. The first involved an Italian peasant, one of the men who came into Rome each day with supplies for the market and often assisted the organisation in transporting men or money. He was captured and tortured by the Gestapo. However, he was promised his freedom if he would lure O'Flaherty out of the Vatican, on the pretext that he wanted to bring the Monsignor to somebody who needed his assistance. The peasant agreed to participate in this scheme. He sent a message that he wanted to see O'Flaherty and was told to call in to St Peter's Square to see the Monsignor. The next day he went into the Vatican where O'Flaherty stood in his usual position at the top of the steps. The square was unusually quiet on that morning at around 8.00 a.m. when the peasant arrived. The Monsignor was able to see a black Gestapo car near the white boundary line between the Vatican and Rome. Also watching was John May who was extremely suspicious that this was a trap and was taking a keen interest in developments. Standing beside were some Swiss Guards who were ready to intervene should the Germans try to cross the boundary. There were three men inside the car. May noticed that, unusually, the engine was kept running. The peasant started to walk across the square, not looking at the Monsignor, but occasionally casting a glance back over his shoulder at the Germans. Three times the peasant approached O'Flaherty, but on the first two occasions he did not look at the Monsignor, and merely walked past. On the third occasion he looked straight at O'Flaherty, and obviously having second thoughts as to the venture he was involved in, immediately turned and ran into a narrow side street beside the Holy Office and made his escape.

The second attempt involved a helper of the organisation named Grossi who had been involved from the very early days. Again the Gestapo had captured him and a combination of torture and bribery persuaded him to agree to betray O'Flaherty. Grossi at that stage was providing a billet for two escapees and Kappler was well aware of that fact. However, he arranged for the accommodation not to be raided to ensure that O'Flaherty would not be alerted to the fact that Grossi was now co-operating with the Gestapo. Grossi came to visit O'Flaherty and told him about escapees who were hiding in a location about thirty miles from Rome. He needed assistance to get them into Rome and he asked for O'Flaherty to go out and visit the group. Grossi informed the Monsignor that one of the escapees was sick and transport would be a problem. Without discussing the case with Derry, O'Flaherty agreed to help by going out to say Mass later that week near where the escapees were hidden and bring back the sick man. The remainder could follow. The day before he was due to go and say the Mass, O'Flaherty was in his room with a couple of his helpers. They were celebrating St Patrick's Day when the phone rang and after listening for a few moments on the phone he was heard to say 'Alright, I understand . . . God forgive him.'[12] The call was a tip-off as to what was planned and so he avoided capture.

Kappler himself took a personal role in the third attempt to capture the Monsignor. He arrived one morning during March with two of his colleagues and examined the situation from the white boundary line. The Monsignor, who was in his usual position, was pointed out to the two men. Kappler explained to them that O'Flaherty was aware of the risk he was running if he came outside Vatican territory and even though he had done so on a significant number of occasions, they had failed to catch him. It was now necessary to lure him across the line. The plan was that the two men would attend Mass themselves later on in the week. On leaving the church through the door near where O'Flaherty regularly stood they were to bustle him across the white line and then let him go. He was then to be shot while escaping. Again, John May came to the rescue. He had got information from a contact named Giuseppe as to just what was planned. (Indeed, it was Giuseppe who had given the tip-off about the previous plan also.) He told John May that an effort would be made to capture and kill the Monsignor but he did not know the details. May suggested that O'Flaherty should stay off the steps and lie low for some time but the Monsignor declined to accept this advice.

> What, me boy and let them think I am afraid? So long as they don't use guns I can tackle any two or three of them with ease, though a scrap would be a bit undignified on the very steps of St Peter's itself, would it not.[13]

The Monsignor was correct in taking this decision. If he disappeared from his usual location for a number of days, or indeed weeks, the problem would only be deferred and was likely to recur when he might not receive advance notice. O'Flaherty and May decided to go ahead and try to use the occasion to teach Kappler a lesson. At the Mass, Giuseppe managed to identify for May the two men. As we have seen, May seemed to have particularly close links with the Swiss Guards and indeed on this occasion they were, to all intents and purposes, following May's orders. The Englishman, in turn, signalled to four Swiss Guards who had appeared just inside the doors of the Basilica. Within a couple of seconds, the Germans found themselves with one Swiss Guard on each side and two behind them. They knew the game was up and left quietly with the Swiss Guards. So the two men and the four Swiss Guards, followed by May, walked out of the Basilica and passed O'Flaherty who at this stage was taking great enjoyment in the proceedings. For the two, there was no particular cause for worry as they presumed they were being escorted back across the white line marking the boundary between the Vatican and Rome. However, May had something else in mind and half way across the Piazza a word from him resulted in a detour being taken down a side street, but still on Vatican land so the German paratroopers on duty on the far side of the line were unable to intervene. In this side street May had arranged for a number of Yugoslav partisans to teach the Gestapo, and indeed Kappler, the lesson that he and O'Flaherty had agreed. They survived but were a very battered and bruised pair, as a result of their experiences, when they reported to Kappler the next morning.

However, the organisation suffered a serious setback when Br Robert was captured. He had been arrested in company with two Italians when he was visiting three American soldiers – Cain, Ashton and Schoenke – and one C. W. Gamble of the Royal Fusiliers, who had been in hiding in the countryside, just outside Rome. The soldiers were placed in a prisoner-of-war camp. The Brother survived because Koch reckoned that, under torture, he might disclose very valuable information. However, Br Robert's past activities as a pastoral clergyman came to his assistance. He told his captors that he had guided two people to an address in Rome at the request of a village priest and that this had been his only involvement. He also suggested that if the Fascist Gestapo cared to check, they would find he was well known to high-ranking German officers. Being a bit nervous of their German superiors, the Fascists checked this out. While working at a hospital run by his order, Br Robert had looked after German patients with as much care and consideration as he had looked after all others. The message came back to Koch that Br Robert had been very helpful to them and that in fact he was needed back at the hospital right away. He was released and once he returned to the hospital, contacted O'Flaherty. The Monsignor arranged for Br Robert to vanish and no member of the organisation met him again until the Germans had left the city. The two Italians were shot a week later, again highlighting the huge risks being taken by those who were helping Monsignor O'Flaherty.

11

Oppression and Fear

Life in Rome was always dangerous for escaped prisoners of war. From time to time the Germans might suddenly cordon off a street and then examine the identity cards of everyone caught in the trap. If they found Italians of military age, these were taken away for deportation to Germany or sent to work in labour camps in the north where the Germans were building defensive positions. Obviously, if an escaped prisoner of war was caught in this situation, he would be sent straight to prison.

One of those who found himself to be the subject of scrutiny by the Germans was Garrad-Cole. He was on a tram one day when he noticed two German soldiers taking a particular interest in him. He got off the tram at the next stop but they followed.

> I tried to convince myself that perhaps it was merely a coincidence that the Germans had left the tram at that point. I stopped to look in a shop window – to see what they would do. Holding my breath, I watched reflections in the window as they passed me. They walked straight on, not even glancing in my direction. I sighed with relief and realised for the first time I was bathed in perspiration. But then they stopped, about twenty yards away to look in another shop window. My heart sank. Obviously, the Huns were playing me at my own game.[1]

He began to run, but very quickly they caught up with him and asked for his identity card. He produced the forged one he had but obviously they doubted its validity and told him they were taking him to prison. And they began to escort him down the street.

> I glanced at my escorts, endeavouring to weigh up my chances. They were armed only with pistols, which they carried in holsters at their waist. They were shorter than myself but quite hefty. My one consolation seemed to lie in the fact that they didn't look particularly bright. Suddenly I struck out my right leg, tripping my right-hand escort so that he staggered forward. As he staggered, I struck him behind the ear with all my might. He fell to the ground. I stepped quickly forward and rushed down the street. A moment later, I heard a bullet whine past my shoulder and saw it strike the wall of a house a few yards ahead of me.[2]

Garrad-Cole knew his only hope was to get off the street or he and maybe innocent civilians would be shot. By chance he was near the apartment block where the Lucidis lived. As he reached the doorway, his pursuers were out of sight and he dived in. Some seconds later they ran past. Upstairs he met Renzo Lucidi who suggested to him that he hide on the roof. When Garrad-Cole got there he realised that he could gain access to the top of the lift so when Renzo Lucidi brought it up to the top floor, 'I climbed on the top of the cage to lie full length in the small space between the top of the cage and the winding gear.'[3] Some minutes later, a German search party arrived and for over an hour sought the escaper without success. However, they had a description of the man they were seeking. After they left, he went to the Lucidis' flat and changed from his light-coloured raincoat and black trilby into a brown overcoat of Renzo's and a brown trilby hat belonging to Gerald, his elder son. The Lucidis sent him on his way with their younger son Maurice, in the belief that he would arouse less suspicion in the company of a child. Maurice and his 'father' walked out of the area with the youngster keeping up a steady chatter so that they aroused nothing more than a glance from the Germans. When they reached the banks of the Tiber and relative safety, Maurice said goodbye and, 'with a cheerful wave went scampering off home'.[4]

When the King and Badoglio's Government deserted Rome in

1943, a secret Committee of National Liberation (CLN) was formed. This was representative of six different political groups and operated under the leadership of Ivane Bonomi. Bonomi was an elder statesman of the Roman scene dating from pre-Mussolini days. His party, the Labour Democrats, were right of centre and opposed to the King and the Badoglio Government which was now located at Brindisi. The most powerful party throughout Italy at that time were the Christian Democrats, led by De Gasperi, representing Catholic and conservative opinion. Also on the right were the Liberal Party and both they and the Christian Democrats were opposed to the King and Badoglio. Even more strongly opposed to them were the three parties of the left, the Party of Action, the Socialist Party and the Communists. Outside the Committee of National Liberation was the Military Front in Rome founded by a Colonel Montezelmo which was supportive of the Monarchy and Badoglio. Linked to the Communist Group was the partisan force known as Gap who were the most effective unit within the Resistance in the ongoing battle with the German and Fascist authorities.

Since the beginning of 1944, the numbers involved in policing Rome and controlling the situation had greatly increased. The Germans had brought in about 500 extra men and, in addition, there was Koch's Special Police Unit and the aggressive new Police Chief, Caruso. Of the 500 additional Germans policing Rome, the Eleventh Company consisted of 160 men and were based in the city centre. They were recent recruits and were undergoing training. Each morning they would march through central Rome to a shooting range and then march back. Aside from anything else, it was a visible presence on the streets of Rome, underlying the intentions of the authorities to control any opposition. They followed this routine day after day from mid-February onwards. One of the Romans who observed their marching and the regularity of the timing was a senior activist in the Gappist movement. He noted that it was almost exactly 2.00 p.m. each day when they turned into the Via Rasella, which is a narrow and steep street up the Quirinal Hill. The partisans decided it was an ideal location for an attack.

The authorities set 23 March as a celebration day in Rome marking the twenty-fifth anniversary of the establishment of the Fascist movement under Mussolini. A range of events was organised for the day. The Gappist leaders selected this as a prime date for launching an attack. Their plan had two targets – one located in a theatre where some of the celebrations were due to be held and the other on the Via Rasella. As it happened, there was a last minute change of plan in relation to the location of the celebration so the former element of the plan had to be aborted. Indeed, the same almost applied to the proposal in relation to the Via Rasella. The police unit did not arrive at 2.00 p.m., as had happened every day previously, because of duties in relation to the celebrations organised elsewhere in the city. The Gappists, who were located at various points of the street to perpetrate the attack, had already decided that if the police unit had not arrived by 4.00 p.m., they would abort. However, the marching policemen arrived into the street at 3.45 p.m. and the Gappists put the plan into action. Essentially it had two elements: firstly, an explosion of TNT by means of a 50-second fuse which would impact on the leading half of the marching group; and secondly, a firing of four 45 mm mortars with a three-second fuse on the latter half of the group. Another group of the partisans were in place to provide cover for the escape of their colleagues. More than two dozen of the policemen were killed instantly. Thirty others lay dying or seriously wounded and two civilians were killed. By 4.00 p.m., all the Gappists had made their escape successfully.

By chance, the journalist, de Wyss, was in the locality. The photographer with whom she worked lived on the Via Rasella and she was bringing him film to develop when a bomb went off.

> There was a terrific explosion, then screams and yells. Then wild machine gun fire made me spin around and run for my life while out of the corner of my eye I saw Germans catching people who tried to escape.[5]

The impact of the 40 lb of dynamite was felt over a wide area, particularly in the Ministry of Corporations where the Fascist commemoration was coming to a close. Many of the senior figures of the German and Fascist organisations were present and immediately made for the scene. People who lived on the street were dragged out and lined up. An observer recorded the scene:

> Germans, Italian soldiers, Fascists and Police were running without reason from one end of the street to the other, observing the roof tops and windows. Some of them were still shooting at those heights. Everyone was shouting, everyone giving orders . . . Germans and Fascists kept bursting into dwellings, dragging out men to the desperate cries of women and children . . . A German General, overcome with convulsive weeping, was running around furiously like a mortally stricken beast.[6]

There was an immediate clash between various high-ranking officials as to what should be done. One wanted to blow up the entire street and indeed engineers arrived to carry out this task. News of the attack reached Hitler's Headquarters by 4.30 p.m. His initial reaction was that the entire quarter of the city, including everyone who lived there, should be blown up and for every German police officer killed they should shoot between 30 and 50 Italians.

Ongoing negotiations between the Vatican and the German Ambassador, as regards Rome becoming an open city, were then reaching a crucial stage. The forthcoming warm weather was expected to facilitate an Allied offensive which might induce Kesselring to abandon his defence in the south and re-establish a new position north of Rome. If successful, the German troops would have withdrawn from the city. The incident put an end to those hopes for the moment. The eventual instruction to Kappler from the German authorities was that for every German killed ten Italians were to be executed. Eventually, 335 were killed. The executions were carried out in the Ardeatine caves and engineers then sealed off the tunnels with explosives. On Saturday 25 March, the newspapers published a communiqué from the German high command:

> On the afternoon of March 23rd criminal elements committed acts of violence by means of bombs against a German column

passing through Via Rasella. In consequence, thirty two members of the German police were killed and a number of them wounded . . . the German High Command is determined to crush the activities of these villainous bandits. No one will be allowed to sabotage the renewed Italo-German co-operation. The Command has ordered that for every German who was murdered, ten of Badoglios communists shall be shot.

This order has been executed.[7]

As Mother Mary observed, a shiver of horror ran through all those who read this cold-blooded communiqué. The Irish observer of these events, MacWhite, reacted similarly:

A Gestapo Officer discussing the matter with the Swiss Chargé d'Affaires elaborated on the efficiency with which the executions were carried out. Efficiency in brutality![8]

(MacWhite, 30 March 1944)

Among those killed were five of O'Flaherty's helpers: Roazzi, Losena, Bernardini, together with Casadi and Fantini who had been captured with Br Robert. After this event, another 2,000 policemen and troops were brought into the city by the Germans to control the situation. Movement through the city now became very difficult. At the same time as the full details of the Ardeatine horror became known throughout the city, the escape organisation found more and more people now willing to help. They were available to assist even though they knew capture would mean immediate death. The CLN had always been racked by dissension and, as Kiernan observed later, the only common denominator among the various parties was their opposition to Fascism. However, this episode brought them together and they managed to agree a statement which was released to the newspapers.

Italian men and women! A crime without a name has been committed in your capital. Under the pretext of a reprisal for an act of war by Italian patriots in which it lost thirty-two of the SS, the enemy has massacred three hundred and twenty innocent persons . . . Rome is horrified by this unprecedented slaughter. It rises in the name of humanity and condemns to

141

abomination the murderers, and equally their accomplices and allies. But Rome will be avenged . . . the blood of our martyrs must not have flowed in vain.[9]

The Monsignor's nephew, Hugh, recalls with fondness two holidays he spent with his uncle in Rome in 1955 and 1959. As with all friends who visited him in the Eternal City, the Monsignor was very generous with his time and expertise in relation to escorting his nephew around the city. However, he rarely spoke of the wartime events. Moreover, there was one place he would bring no visitor to and that was the Caves, although he would arrange for somebody else to do so. His nephew surmises:

I think he had lost too many friends there and might have the idea that, if he had been captured by the Germans, he would have been consigned there too.[10]

We know, however, that he did make one visit. Immediately after Liberation, the Ardeatine Caves became a location of investigation and subsequently pilgrimage. The US authorities appointed a commission of American and Italian officials to investigate the crime and to exhume the bodies and identify them insofar as this was possible. When that was complete, the location was open to family members and others who wished to come. O'Flaherty came on a visit in 1947, in the company of Veronica Dunne, the renowned singer and music teacher who, at that stage, was living in Rome, as a student under his guardianship. She recalls his tears during that visit as they knelt on the floor of the caves and together recited the Rosary for those who had been murdered.

After the massacre at the Caves, more people were willing to offer their assistance. One source of additional help came through Giuseppe, who had been valuable in tipping off the organisation about the attempted snatches of Monsignor O'Flaherty, as we have seen. He had a friend who worked as a clerk in the police headquarters. This in fact was the lame Italian boy who had twice tipped off Mrs Chevalier with accurate information. Both youths wanted to enter into an arrangement, for a small payment, whereby prior notice of the routine orders for the German and Fascist Gestapo groups would be supplied to O'Flaherty and Derry.

For the remainder of the time the organisation was in operation this information proved to be highly accurate and valuable. In fact, this offer of additional help came just in the nick of time as it became obvious that somebody was leaking information about the organisation. O'Flaherty's team of priests and Simpson were kept busy travelling through the city moving people, often with only an hour or two to spare. Keeping 'ahead of the posse' was enormously difficult as the routine orders were published usually about midday. Then they had to be transferred to the British Legation by a circuitous route where, depending on the information supplied, Derry had to put emergency evacuation procedures into action. As well as forewarning them of moves the security forces were about to make, Giuseppe was in a position to tip off the organisation about information being supplied by those supportive of the authorities in relation to people on the run.

> As a result of several denouncements, the Via Merulana is being closely watched these days since British and American ex PW are reported to be hidden there. Houses will shortly be searched. House number 181 is under suspicion . . . An anonymous denouncement has been filed at the central police headquarters stating the presence of a New Zealand prisoner in a house of the Via Collegio Romano.[11]

Even more interestingly he reports on likely sources of help. For example he supplied information to Derry in relation to one Pizzirani, head of the political office.

> I am informed that PIZZIRANI . . . can be easily bribed since he realises that Rome will shortly fall into Allied hands and he wants to make all his various activities as lucrative as possible before he has to leave the capital . . . PIZZIRANI is willing to annul all the documents relative to the ex PW and to avoid obeying any orders for the rounding-up of ex PW – or at least to see that these orders are not carried out with the expected results desired by the German and Fascist police. He asks 50,000 Lire for this. Our informer who acts as go between wants 10,000 Lire for himself.[12]

Giuseppe was also able to confirm a suspicion which Derry had that the Germans were now sending out agents dressed as priests in an effort to get in touch with British escapees. Eventually de Vial made his way from the French Embassy to visit Derry and reported that Perfetti, who had met Derry when he first arrived in Rome, was the betrayer. He had been in the organisation from its earliest days and knew the whereabouts of a large number of billets. It seems he had been arrested, handed over to Koch and had cracked under torture. Not only had he guided Koch and his men to the hideouts, but he had operated the secret signal to gain admission. Within a few days, 21 escapees had been recaptured and more than a dozen Italians who were hiding them had been arrested.

By this time, John Furman had moved to live with the family of Romeo Giuliani and his wife, together with their three daughters and two sons, on the Via Buonarroti near the Basilica of Santa Maria Maggiore, which meant he was nearer those for whom he was caring. One of the sons, Gino, eighteen years of age, became a very valuable assistant for Furman. He and his friend Memo were set the task of finding new billets. They found some outside the city but the situation was getting more difficult within it. The rationing system, which had never been very efficient, had more or less broken down completely and it was now costing a lot of money to keep escapees and evaders within Rome. Eventually additional funds were made available which relieved the situation to some extent. They secured two new billets through the help of Theresa, a friend of Mrs Chevalier, and Signor Pediconi, solicitor to Nini Pallavicini, who was still in hiding in the German College.

On hearing that Perfetti had been arrested, Gino told Furman that he knew him. Furman instantly sensed danger and moved to another location but, when nothing happened, returned to the Giuliani home on 5 April. He happened to be out on 7 April when the Fascists arrived and arrested both father and son. Again under torture, the boy cracked and began to leak information. Of all the billets he knew about, only two were not raided during this period. Simpson meanwhile, unaware of this problem, had gone to the flat which a few weeks previously had been used as a clearing house to which the Monsignor sent all new arrivals. This was located in the basement of a block of flats which the Vatican used to house some of its officials and it was located less than 100 yards from St Peter's Square. Furman recalls:

> The porter, Paolino, in his forties, was a sprightly tiny man, perhaps four feet six inches in height. His heart, however, was as big as his stature was small. Although the accommodation available for his wife and small children was extremely limited, he, nevertheless, accepted whomever the Monsignor might send him. At times, as many as seven British, Dominion or American soldiers would be in hiding there. It was part of the arrangement that no prisoner should be kept there for more than two or three nights, so that space should be available for new arrivals.[13]

On arrival, Furman found that the Fascists had already called and dragged Paolino away but the five British escapees were still there. In the few moments before he opened the door, Paolino had the presence of mind to put the five into a cellar and push his bed over the trapdoor entrance. Simpson immediately moved these five to other billets. Derry and O'Flaherty were very concerned to note that these arrests were moving closer to the Chevalier apartment. As a result of the increased level of activity by the security forces, an instruction was sent to Furman and Simpson to move around carefully and with extra caution. Simpson never received this message. He simply vanished. His involvement in the organisation was such that he had been ordered never to spend two successive nights at the same location. He was staying with the American lieutenant, Dukate, on 18 April when the Germans raided during the night and arrested him. By this time, Simpson was using new identity cards which O'Flaherty had provided, naming him as William O'Flynn, an Irish citizen employed in the Vatican Library. Notwithstanding this, Dukate and Simpson were placed under arrest and taken from the premises. They were put in the back seat of a German car and two German Gestapo men sat on top of them. Simpson and Dukate both had documents on them that might have proved incriminating had they been discovered. As it happened, the window of the car on Simpson's side was partially open. He managed to extract his wallet including the documents and 8,000 lire, and push it out through the window without being seen.

> I prayed that some thoroughly dishonest person would pick it up and, in order to keep the money, would not hand it over to the police. In Rome right now the prayer had a strong chance of being answered.[14]

In the same way he then managed to get rid of 5,000 lire and some papers which Dukate was carrying. Within a few minutes they had arrived at the Regina Coeli prison.

Giuseppe could not get any information about Simpson from his sources. By the same token, Molly Stanley's visits to the prison had no success. Even an intervention by a film star, Flora Volpini, in whose apartment both Furman and Simspon had stayed at various times, was unsuccessful. She went to visit the Governor of the Regina Coeli prison, who was an old friend of hers, but he had no knowledge of any prisoner named Simpson. It emerged later that Simpson was using the false name from his forged identity cards.

In a letter back to the Dublin authorities, MacWhite casts a clinical eye on recent events:

> In its long history and throughout its many vicissitudes it would be difficult to find a parallel for the Rome of today. It has over two million inhabitants – a fourth of whom are refugees from the war zone or from bombed out homes . . . the bread ration has been reduced to three and a half ounces per day and no pasta has been distributed since February. How the people live is a mystery . . . there are several political parties the best organised and strongest of which is the communist. A number of clandestine newspapers are also published . . . The average Roman is and always has been an individualist. He goes his own way indifferent to the fate of his neighbours . . . The Romans will tolerate any form of government or any system of tyranny for a certain time. They will accept whatever profit may be derived from them. Many a time they rallied in the Piazza Venezia to cheer the Duce then return to their

favourite café where they dammed Fascism for the rest of the day. Any form of discipline is repugnant to them and that is probably the main reason why the Germans who walk on the dotted line fail to understand or subdue them. The Roman emperors were psychologists, hence their policy of *panem et circenses*. The Italians ate the bread, enjoyed the games but have not succeeded in doing anything particularly noteworthy since the battle of Actium . . .[15]

(*MacWhite*, 3 April 1944)

In these final weeks of the German occupation the mood in the city was changing, as Mother Mary notes:

German women in Rome had orders to leave the city today; a significant detail if nothing else. They say that the Gestapo is going also; is it possible?[16]

(*Mother Mary St Luke*, 29 April 1944)

Every day we expect the invasion. Every day we listen to victory talk on the wireless. Every day we notice growing tension around us, and ill-concealed hopes of the arrival of the Allies. When will they come?[17]

(*Mother Mary St Luke*, 7 May 1944)

A real event took place today: we each had our monthly ration of 3½ oz. of meat for dinner. It looked and tasted like donkey meat, but it may really have been something better.[18]

(*Mother Mary St Luke*, 8 May 1944)

She and the members of her congregation, together with the evaders they were housing, numbering about 40 in all, were facing the same difficult circumstances in relation to food supply as the rest of the residents of Rome. While her diary entry of 8 May shows that she had not lost her sense of humour in dealing with this deprivation, the evidence is even stronger in the next:

Our cat ate a rat. No, this is not turning into a kindergarten text book. He was just making history. The point is that he is, like most cats who live in houses, thoroughly spoiled. He is lordly, lazy and proud. He will only eat a mouse if it is young and tender. In the way of other eatables, what we get he shares. Today, however, his whole being rose up against a diet of macaroni, dried peas and rice, cooked in water with no cheese, no butter, no gravy, no milk. With grim determination he withdrew to the cellar, killed and ate a big rat – all except the tail, which we think he is going to appeal to the cook to make into soup for him. This historical fact that he was underlining is that food conditions are bad in Rome at present.[19]

(*Mother Mary St Luke*, 9 May 1944)

The authorities made other moves now to put O'Flaherty and Derry on the defensive. The period from mid-March to early May was very difficult and 46 men they had been catering for were either re-arrested or shot. In addition, the food situation was very difficult. Ninety per cent of supplies were now on the black market and prices had increased tenfold since November. The official ration of bread was about two slices per day. There were riots in bakeries and lorries carrying food were attacked. Strong pressure was also brought to bear on the Swiss Government by the German authorities and all aid from the Swiss Legation ceased. It had been made clear to the Swiss authorities that the Germans knew perfectly well they were assisting escaped Allied prisoners of war and, if this did not stop, their diplomatic staff would be arrested. This would have been very easy as the Swiss representatives were still in the Italian part of Rome. They had never relocated to the Vatican as it was unnecessary for them, being representatives of a neutral country. Then Ambassador von Weizsaecker made representations to the Heads of some of the religious orders in Rome, and Frs Borg, Madden and Buckley were confined to their houses. The organisation was now facing a lot of day-to-day difficulties. Frs Borg, Madden and Buckley were unable to be of assistance. Monsignor O'Flaherty was restricted to the Vatican and any departure from that arrangement represented the most incredible risk. Br Robert was in retirement and Joe Pollak was of limited assistance because of ill-health.

As a result of the increased level of partisan activity, the work was becoming more difficult. The number of German security police increased and Koch's gang became even more active. Feeding prisoners was now more difficult because of the increasing cost and the decline in availability of food. This increased pressure on the organisation caused Derry to issue instructions tightening up security. He reviewed recent events:

1. A large number (over forty) ex PW have been retaken in the last few weeks in ROME. Of these, twenty-eight were recaptured as a result of denunciations, and sixteen have been picked up in the street (of these sixteen, three were picked up in a drunken condition).

2. Current propaganda in ROME is that the Allies will not arrive before the Autumn. This is strong propaganda when coupled with the food shortage and with the static condition of the bridge-head and CASSINO fronts.

3. The Fascists and German SS have been, during the last four weeks, and still are far more active in the respect of the rounding up of Allied ex PW that any time since the Armistice.

As a result of this assessment of the situation he highlighted a number of conclusions.

1. Fascist gangs, working in collaboration with the Gestapo, are out to make a name for themselves by rounding up all ex PW in ROME.

2. The work of finding billets, paying padrones, contacting and supplying our men is more difficult than ever before.

3. The longer men remain cooped up in-doors, the more desperate becomes their attitude of mind and stimulated by a drink or two, the more likely they are to take ill-advised action.

He then went on to issue instructions.

1. No more ex PW are to be billeted in ROME. Any arriving in the city will be given financial assistance and advised to return to the country.

2. Ex PW must on no account leave their billets unless they

receive warning of an imminent raid. <u>The practice of going from one billet to another to visit friends must cease forthwith</u>.

3. If forced to 'make a run' for it, ex PW must leave ROME and hide out in the country. Dashing to another billet only compromises additional people.[20]

In the second week of May the 'Schoolmaster' was arrested. Fernando Giustini was a village schoolmaster in the village of Corchiano which is located in Viterbo province. He had lived as a child for a short time in the United States. During the War, he led a band of partisans in his region, who accomplished acts of sabotage against the military occupying the area, but who also were of assistance to people on the run, notably prisoners of war. In this latter aspect of his activities, he worked with O'Flaherty and his organisation. His link with O'Flaherty was through another Irish priest, Fr Clancy, who was then Director of the Collegio Marcantonio Colonna. The German authorities became aware of his work in Corchiano and carried out a house-to-house search. All members of the family were able to escape. They came to Rome where O'Flaherty and his colleagues managed to hide the mother, two sons and one daughter. Fernando continued his activity in Rome until such time as he was picked up as well. He also was tortured but did not disclose any information and eventually managed to make his escape.

On top of all of that, Simpson had disappeared. A heavier load now fell on John Furman but he was becoming too well known. He dyed his hair jet black and changed the position of his hair parting. This, together with the shaving off of his moustache, altered his appearance and he now looked like a fairly typical Italian. Within a couple of days, he met a friend who was able to tell him that the authorities had identified him as the most important person regularly out and about on the streets of Rome for them to capture next. Renzo Lucidi stepped into the breach and devoted himself full time to the work of the organisation. Whenever there was a warning that it was dangerous for Furman to be out on the streets, Renzo and his wife Adrienne dealt with all deliveries of money and supplies to escapees. Things were getting very difficult in the city because there was a rash of minor explosions, assassinations and other events as the running battle between the authorities and the resistance developed.

One of the helpers, Giovanni Cecarelli, was looking after five men who had been evacuated from Mrs Chevalier's flat. All five were at home when the Fascist Gestapo hammered on his door. As there was no other exit, he bundled them through the French window onto the tiny balcony outside and drew the curtain across. He admitted the raiding party who searched the flat and found nothing incriminating, but just as they were leaving, the sergeant pointed to the French window and demanded to know what was through there. 'Only the balcony', said Giovanni and, in an effort to distract the sergeant, offered him a drink. However, the sergeant decided to go through with a routine check of the balcony but, much to Giovanni's surprise, returned a few seconds later and asked for the drink. After the Fascists had gone, Giovanni went out on the balcony and was surprised to see nothing. He owed his life to the fact that he routinely stored a ladder on the balcony and the five had climbed up to the balcony above and pulled the ladder up with them.

Despite all this, the organisation was very active. The income for that month was in excess of 2,750,000 lire (approximately €350,000 in current terms), consisting of about 250,000 lire from Tittmann and the balance from Sir D'Arcy. Derry's careful accounts show that the money was spent on 164 escaped prisoners of war who were being catered for in Rome and in excess of 3,500 in the countryside around. These latter escapees were in 32 different locations with the groups varying in size from 3 to 110.

12

The Liberation

The difficulties the organisation had experienced in recent weeks continued into the month of May, while at the same time, the numbers seeking their assistance were increasing by about a hundred per week. The Monsignor was called to a meeting with His Holiness.

> I have heard today from an Italian source that Monsignor O'Flaherty of the Holy Office has been requested by the Holy Father not to leave the Vatican City and to give an undertaking that he would abstain from all activities in relation to providing shelter or money for escaped British prisoners of war. He is known to have boasted some months ago that Prince Doria had placed a couple of million lire at his disposal for this purpose. The Germans apparently got to know of his activities for, several months ago, the Secretary of the German Embassy to the Holy See asked Kiernan if he knew a certain Monsignor O'Flaherty in Rome. Very likely they protested to the Vatican which provoked papal restrictions on his movements. His actions were not in accord either with the neutral character of the Vatican City or of the country of which he is a citizen.[1]
>
> (MacWhite, 9 May 1944)

It seems reasonable to assume that this report is relatively accurate. However, it would be wrong to take that as evidence of papal disapproval. After all, at this stage the Allies were weeks away, though as it turned out it took longer for them to arrive than anticipated. During the entire period of his activities, O'Flaherty's life was in danger. In addition, of course, the Pope would have been concerned about the inevitable embarrassment that would have been caused had the Monsignor been captured. The most likely explanation of this meeting is that that Pope had decided O'Flaherty should run no more risks. The person best placed to judge O'Flaherty's position throughout this period was his closest associate, Sam Derry. The Englishman's consistent view was that the Monsignor had the tacit approval of the Pope for what he was doing and there is no reason to doubt the accuracy of that observation.

At the same time, controls on visitors to the Vatican were tightened up and it was not possible to gain access to Monsignor O'Flaherty in the German College. Yet again, John May and his unusual relationship with the Swiss Guard came to the rescue.

> He induced the Swiss Guards to allow specified people to make use of the guard-room by the Santa Marta gate. On arrival at the Vatican, we went straight to the guard-room. One of the guards telephoned John on the internal phone and he came down. In a quiet corner of the room we transacted our business with relative privacy.[2]

May then would pass on whatever messages were necessary to Monsignor O'Flaherty or indeed bring him down to meet the visitors if that was needed.

On 12 May, the Allied Forces opened a major new offensive on the southern front.

> The offensive has put new life into us, and new hope into the Italians. The Allies are progressing slowly, but as long as they do progress, all is well.[3]
>
> (*Mother Mary St Luke*, 14 May 1944)

> People in Rome can talk of nothing else than the offensive and are already settling dates for the arrival of the Allies – as they have so often done in the past.[4]
>
> (*Mother Mary St Luke*, 19 May 1944)

High Fascist officials are known to have completed preparations for leaving Rome. The Chief of the Fascist police, the party leaders . . . have already parked luggage which only await the signal. In German circles it is said they will abandon the city on the day the Allies attempt a landing . . . which they anticipate on May 22nd or thereabouts.[5]

(*MacWhite*, 20 May 1944)

We hear that Kesselring has called up all his available reserves . . . Rome is tense. The Romans are in high spirits, but they dread what the Germans may do before they go . . . The panic that is beginning to show itself recalls the panic last September when Rome was occupied. Anxiety to conceal young men who are wanted by the Fascists for the army or forced labour, and desire to protect their families, in case of reprisals, is increased by the knowledge that tomorrow at midnight the time 'graciously granted by Il Duce to defaulters for military service' expires. For weeks press and radio have never ceased to advise, order, coax, beg, encourage and direct defaulters to come and be forgiven, to join the ranks of the Republican army, assuring them that they would suffer no penalty for delay until midnight on May 25th. After that they would be searched out, arrested and shot in the back as deserters.[6]

(*Mother Mary St Luke*, 23 May 1944)

Derry was afraid that escapees, hearing what was going on, would now begin to engage in rash actions, such as coming out of hiding to try and join the battle. So he issued strict instructions for all to stay in their accommodations. Not all obeyed and two decided to visit Mrs Chevalier to get a good meal. She was renowned for the quality of catering provided to escapees. There were no longer any soldiers billeted there but it acted as a clearing house on occasions and as a general base for food distribution. However, the family were aware that the house was under observation. Two German SS men, who were regularly on the street, had questioned the caretaker Egidio about the inhabitants of Apartment 9 (Mrs Chevalier's) and she subsequently telephoned O'Flaherty warning him that she was now under full-time observation. Furman passed a message to all escapees who knew her to stay away from the apartment but presumably these two, Martin and Everett, did not get the warning. When they knocked at her apartment door she was horrified and told them to go away immediately as the Germans were watching. They knew that to go back downstairs was to face the likelihood of immediate arrest. They also knew their first duty was to Mrs Chevalier so they went down the flight of stairs as quickly as possible. Her quick warning had bought them some time. But as they turned into the street, one of the Germans left the café opposite and followed them.

> Fifty yards from Mrs M's house was a block of flats through whose courtyard one could pass to emerge into another street. The two boys aware that they were being followed, entered the courtyard and then ran. For two or three days, I heard nothing of them. I had already given them up for lost, when I discovered that they were safely hid away in a billet of whose existence I had been unaware.[7]

Furman reported this episode to O'Flaherty who immediately decided the situation was getting too close for comfort and arrangements were made to evacuate Mrs Chevalier and her family. One at a time, at brief intervals, without baggage of any sort, the members of her family including herself left the premises. It did not occur to the watching SS men that an entire family was abandoning its accommodation. Presumably they were looking out for clearly identifiable Allied ex-prisoners. By different routes, the various members of the family made their way to the home of a friend a distance away and eventually the whole family moved to a farm on the outskirts of the city where they remained until the Germans had left Rome. Furman recalls the Maltese widow:

> What can be said of this incredible woman, who I guessed to be in her early forties? I would not call her brave for it seemed to me that she had no conception of fear. Her kindness and generosity were unparalleled, her maternal spirit and compassion boundless. During my stay in Rome some scores of Allied prisoners must have received hospitality in her home.[8]

Fr Anselmo Musters (Dutchpa) was a native of Holland and had been one of O'Flaherty's earliest recruits. His arrest was perhaps one of the things O'Flaherty dreaded most and it occurred on the first day of May. He had just left the billet where a South African sergeant, Carl Schwabe, was located, when he became aware that he was being followed. He stopped for a moment and his follower stopped too, looking fairly suspiciously into a shop window. Fr Musters strolled on but changed direction and made for the Basilica of Santa Maria Maggiore. Before he reached the church, the plain-clothes man overtook him and demanded identity documents. The Dutch priest attempted to gain the sanctuary of the church but the policeman jumped in front of him, pulled a pistol from inside his coat and demanded that he stop. Fr Musters pushed him aside but then he felt a vicious blow to the back of his head and he crumbled. A Palatine guard, who from within the church had seen the attack, rushed forward and dragged the semi-conscious priest inside. The German soldier disappeared. Contact was made with the Vatican authorities who instructed Fr Musters to stay where he was until the following morning when he would be collected by an escort and taken back to his mother house. It was presumed he was safe in the church but this was not the case.

> About half an hour later the Church was surrounded by German SS men, and party under a Captain KEHLE entered the room where Father ANSELMO was. As Father ANSELMO refused to accompany the SS men, he was struck on the head by KEHLE with a sub-machine gun, and received a wound which did not heal for a fortnight. He was dragged by the feet out of the extra territorial property, down the steps and taken to Via Tasso. His arrival there created quite an atmosphere of triumph because the Germans thought that they had arrested an English Colonel disguised as a priest. His clothes were torn from him and thoroughly searched, all the seams of his garments were opened up, and his shoes were taken to pieces. His hands were handcuffed behind his back, and his feet also manacled.[9]

He was interrogated daily in the prison on the Via Tasso for over a fortnight by two members of the Gestapo, Captains Schulz and Wolf, who questioned him endlessly about the organisation which they knew existed to assist Allied ex-prisoners of war. They even produced a diagram which outlined the structure of the organisation. He was shocked to see that it was very accurate. However, through the two weeks of physical and mental abuse, he maintained he knew nothing about the organisation. Eventually his captors admitted defeat and threw him into a dark cell where he remained for another fortnight. The plan was to send him to Germany and so he was put on a train. His likely fate, had he arrived in Germany, was fairly clear. However, the train halted at Florence and he managed to make a getaway and he returned to Rome immediately.

A couple of days after Fr Musters had been arrested, Furman very nearly joined him in captivity. He was travelling on a tram when it was raided by the SS. He was delivering money and tobacco to various billets. The cellophane-wrapped tobacco was an American troops issue captured by the Germans and sold on the black market where it had been bought by those working for O'Flaherty's organisation. His last visit before he got on the tram was to Johnny Johnstone who had now moved into a Vatican-owned block of flats in Trastevere, one of the toughest quarters of Rome 'where he was guest of Monsignor Giobbelina, a friar tuck of a man. Living in the same block, with different families were three South Africans and Garrad-Cole.'[10] He then hopped on a tram which was subsequently stopped by a cordon of Fascist soldiers.

> My heart sank and inwardly I cursed and cursed and cursed. To be picked up again in so short a time before liberation![11]

The soldiers in the street had formed a line from the front door of the tram to the entrance of one of the block of flats and the intention was to shepherd the men in there and allow the women and children go free.

> At the first sign of danger, I had extracted from my breast-pocket my tell-tale notebook with [its] code entries and statement of money spent. I was standing near the front end

of the tram and the pressure of people moving up behind me was impelling me towards the exit. Just in time, a man sitting on my left rose from his place, pushed past me and left the tram. I plunged into a seat, tore the offending pages from my notebook to the mystification of the woman next to me, screwed them into a tight ball and dropped them, unseen, into her shopping basket.[12]

In total, 40 men were removed from the train, including Furman. As he moved in the line for questioning he had managed to break open the tobacco in his pockets from its cellophane and dispose of the tell-tale wrappings. Just as it was his turn to be questioned he recollected the small Union Jack badge which he invariably wore under his lapel. It was too late to do anything about it then.

My identity card was one issued by the Vatican City State and ostensibly signed by the Governor but, I regret, without his knowledge or authority. The accompanying document was a certificate from the Vatican to the effect that I was an employee there in the Office of Technical Services. The soldiers had probably never seen documents like it before; few people had. The power of the Vatican![13]

The documents which had been forged by Princess Nini were of high quality and managed to ensure his release.

On 18 May, the Allied Forces took Cassino and with that, it became clear a significant turn in the War had taken place.

Explosions and the sound of artillery reaches us fitfully by night and by day at present . . . Late yesterday evening even more refugees came, having escaped from the concentration camp, like the others. Then this morning, still more fleeing from the renewed bombing at Frascati – men, women and children.[14]

(*Mother Mary St Luke*, 25 May 1944)

Hope rises as the Allies progress. We have waited for over eight months, but now every added hour seems interminable . . . The threatened search for patriots, from house to house, is not taking place after all. And for an excellent reason. No one would undertake it . . . they were afraid. Popular feeling is running high, the patriots are armed and have plenty of ammunition, and a popular rising might easily follow police action of that sort. No one wanted to put a match to that particular powder barrel, above all with the Allies thundering, as it were, at the gates of the city. So the terrible threat formulated from after midnight on May 25th has come to nothing like so many other Fascist undertakings.[15]

(*Mother Mary St Luke*, 27 May 1944)

The sound of war continues to echo around us day and night, but unusually continuous pounding of guns in the Alban hills began to be heard about mid day. The electric current for such buses and trams as remained to us was cut off this morning, so one has to walk or not go at all. It is really better for everyone to stay indoors, especially the men.[16]

(*Mother Mary St Luke*, 29 May 1944)

As the month of May draws to a close the people of Rome anxiously await the arrival of the Allies. The City maintains its traditional calm and sober elements of the population are doing their utmost to get the public to avoid hostile demonstrations towards the occupation authorities. The Gestapo has all but disappeared from the streets and one rarely sees a German soldier these days.[17]

(*MacWhite*, 31 May 1944)

In the meantime, Furman had decided that he had been over-optimistic in anticipating the arrival of Allied soldiers, and mindful of the necessity to account for money, sent a note to Sam Derry on 29 May:

I am very much afraid that we shall have to pay out again for June – at any rate, for half the month. What a pity! All my bets were to the effect that they would be here this month.[18]

Suddenly everyone wanted to help but way 'ahead of the posse' was the double agent, Cipolla. The big fear at this stage was that the Germans, enraged by the turn of events, would start to shift all the prisoners out of Rome to concentration camps or even shoot them. Adrienne Lucidi came up with the answer. She was aware that Cipolla wanted to get into the Allies' good books as quickly as he could. She proposed that they give him his chance by instructing him to tell the Germans that he had made contact with the escape organisation and would be in a position to infiltrate it if he could get Simpson released as an earnest of good faith. It was decided that Cipolla should ask for the release of two prisoners of his choice. If this request was granted, he was to endeavour to secure the freedom of Simpson and a Captain John Armstrong who had been in the prison for about nine months. The Germans agreed and supplied Cipolla with a list of British prisoners. Neither name was on it. All he could do was pick two names at random, and to their great surprise, two English civilians who had been jailed since Italy entered the War found themselves free. The problem still remained to find Simpson and Armstrong. Blon Kiernan, the Irish Ambassador's daughter, had friends in the German Legation whom she visited regularly and she was often used as a source of information by O'Flaherty. She was able to advise that the Germans had been making enquiries at the Irish Legation about an Irishman named William O'Flynn and the Legation had replied, as was the case, that they knew nothing about him. Just then, through a cousin of one of his cellmates who was acting as the prison doctor, Simpson had managed to smuggle out information that he was in the prison and was using the name William O'Flynn. The organisation could not work out any way of being of assistance to him. Obviously no diplomatic intercession could be made now without confirming that he was a British officer with a false identity which would give the authorities every excuse for executing him as a spy.

As happened so often, something unusual turned up. O'Flaherty was at work in the Holy Office one morning when he was told a Roman nobleman wished to see him. The nobleman reminded O'Flaherty of the episode when he had rescued a girl by making her a temporary and informal member of the Swiss Guard in order to smuggle her to safety. There was some polite conversation as to how the girl had got on subsequently and O'Flaherty was pleased to hear that she was safe and well.

However, the next comment surprised the Monsignor when the nobleman indicated that he had come seeking the Monsignor's help on behalf of Pietro Koch, one of his mortal enemies. However, the nobleman was quick to emphasise that he was not seeking direct assistance for Koch, who realised what his fate would be when the Allies took over. The request was that the Monsignor would assist Koch's wife and mother, in return for which Koch would ensure that all the Monsignor's friends were left in Regina Coeli, instead of being transported to Germany. The Monsignor agreed to help but set down a condition that as evidence of good faith Koch would have to deliver safely the two British officers in Regina Coeli, Simpson and Armstrong. He undertook to make arrangements to assist the wife and mother if this was carried out. Sitting in his cell the next day, Simpson heard the name 'Lieutenant Simpson' called out but at this stage he did not know whether it was a trap or not; similarly with Armstrong, so neither responded to the call. This placed O'Flaherty in an exceptionally awkward position. When the nobleman returned and told him nobody had come forward he asked that Koch be informed that Simpson would be found under the name of O'Flynn but as regards Armstrong it was not known what alias he was using. Koch was given this message, but things were happening too quickly now, and so neither was released.

> A fresh rumour – optimistic, this time – says insistently that the Pope has promised the Germans that, if they do no damage to the city as they withdraw, he will make himself responsible for all their wounded whom they might leave behind; reports as to the number of wounded vary between 20,000 and 40,000 . . . We are immensely cheered by the news, broadcast from Anzio, that the Allies are bringing to Rome foodstuffs of every kind except flour and oil . . . lack of food has had an alarming slimming effect on everyone in Rome, not only the poor, but on the man-in-the-street and one's friends. It gives one a heartache to see it. No longer is it complimentary to allude the loss of weight; on the contrary, the subject is tactfully avoided.[19]
>
> (*Mother Mary St Luke*, 31 May 1944)

It is said that last night the Pope sent for the German Ambassador, and kept him from 11.00 p.m. until 1.00 a.m. talking about the possibilities of not defending Rome, once the Allies had broken through their line in the Castelli and of not destroying the city as they withdrew. It is understood that the Pope was in a large measure successful.[20]

(*Mother Mary St Luke*, 2 June 1944)

The Allies are pouring into the plain that surrounds Rome like water through a dyke . . . Although many Germans left yesterday, at present the hotels near the station are crowded with them . . . All last night heavy vehicles, tanks and lorries rumbled through the street.[21]

(*Mother Mary St Luke*, 3 June 1944)

A British army advance party had reached the Pope's villa at Castelgandolfo and had made radio contact with Derry. Liberation was only hours away. Amid a constant barrage of guns the Germans started to pull out. In the meantime, O'Flaherty, following his policy of always giving assistance to anyone in need, had begun to make arrangements for the safety of the wife and mother of Koch. They were to be taken to Naples and given shelter in a convent but they both refused this offer of assistance, deciding instead to try and make their own escape.

Of particular concern during those final days were the Russians. Of all those who had opposed them, the Germans reserved their most deep-seated hatred for the Russian army. There were in excess of 400 escaped Russian prisoners of war hidden in and around Rome by the organisation in late May 1944. The fear was that these were the people most at risk of last-minute reprisals by the Germans, if they were located. A student in the mother house of the Jesuit order, just beside St Peter's, approached Fr Joy who he knew was a friend of O'Flaherty's. Joy and O'Flaherty were both trained in the Jesuit Mungret College but Joy had not been involved in the escape organisation. His work in Rome was in a secretariat which had been devised to fight world Communism. The student explained to Fr Joy that, while those hidden in the Russian College were probably safe enough, those in the private accommodation could be at risk. Fr Joy immediately approached the Monsignor for help, whose response was, 'Of course we must help them, Francis. Stay here for a moment.'[22]

O'Flaherty went across to Derry and explained the situation.

> Have you got any cash about, me boy? I have a wee problem. We want to shift some Russians to make sure these Germans don't get 'em, but the landladies want their money first![23]

Derry immediately produced the equivalent of £400 in lire. 'I hope Joe Stalin pays it back.'[24] Immediately, the organisation swung into action on that first weekend in June and all the Russians who were in billets throughout the city were re-located as a precautionary measure.

Field Marshal Kesselring was one of Germany's most talented military strategists. He had particular talents in deploying the troops available to him in a defensive position and then, when appropriate, conducting an orderly withdrawal. He realised from the outset that defending Italy south of Rome was something he could not sustain in the long term but he had persuaded Hitler that this was the right strategy to adopt. The objective was to make the Allies pay very dearly for every inch of ground they gained in Italy and indeed he proved to be very successful in the implementation of this policy. Falling back from that position, he could easily have made Rome a battleground, in such a way that the experiences of the city of Stalingrad might have been repeated. Hitler had sent orders to Kesselring at midnight on 3 June, ordering him to defend the city at all costs and to blow up the Tiber bridges. Mussolini had sent a message to Kesselring making the same request. However, it seems Kesselring had already decided to withdraw. All day on 3 June, while the Fascists were making preparation to clear out of the city, Kesselring continued to move men and material to the front to give the appearance of continuing the fight. He arranged for a large number of his senior officers to attend the opera that night. Von Weizsaecker, at his request, went to the Vatican at 10.30 p.m. to meet with Montini and Tardini. His message was that Kesselring wanted to save Rome and he was hoping that the Vatican would intercede with the Allies to hold off on their attack. Essentially, this was a ploy to create a safe corridor of retreat for the Germans, but the Vatican diplomats refused to play their part. In the meantime, circumstances within the prison were changing. Simpson and Dukate had been questioned endlessly during the month of May. The fact that they had nothing in their possession other than a small amount of cash was to their advantage and they realised how lucky they had been to have got rid of the incriminating items in their wallets. Dukate maintained he was Italian and his papers supported that. Simpson's claim that he was Irish was reflected in his documents. However, his questioners clearly had an idea who he was. Eventually, they checked with the Irish Legation and asked if they knew of a Vatican employee called William O'Flynn. It was confirmed that there was such an employee, a priest, and he was currently in the Vatican. On 30 May, the prisoners were able to hear gunfire, distant but unmistakable, and they realised that the circumstances outside were altering radically. On that day also, a new squad of military police arrived to take over control of the prison and it was quickly realised that these were Austrians. The Germans were gone. Within a couple of days, the prison gates were open and hundreds were released. Derry's careful accounts show that a considerable sum of money was spent on bribery during this period. That morning, Furman had called to Renzo Lucidi's flat. They had arranged to meet to work out their accounts but he recalls that concentration was difficult.

> History was being made at our very door; the importance of our additions and subtractions paled into insignificance. We sat up, startled, as the door bell sounded our old familiar signal; for the last month or more we had used a new ring. Could this be a trap, a last minute effort by the Gestapo or Koch's gang? We waited tensely while Peppina opened the door. We heard a scream.[25]

In fact it was Simpson, who had walked to freedom from the prison.

As they left the prison, the Gestapo took with them fourteen prisoners of war as hostages. However, they swiftly concluded that minding those prisoners on the journey north was a handicap and they were unloaded near the Rome suburb of Lastorta and executed on 4 June. The bodies were discovered by local people and, after a funeral service, buried some days later. A remembrance service is held on that day each year at the site. A memorial has been erected containing the names of some of those executed. However, one plaque refers to 'the unknown Englishman'. Research completed in March of 2007 fairly conclusively suggested this, in fact, is the grave of Captain Armstrong, whom O'Flaherty so nearly rescued. However, there are now suggestions that his name was not Armstrong but in fact he was a secret agent working under the code name 'Gabriel'.

> With admirable restraint, the Romans looked on, spectators of the reverse of what they had seen in September: the boot was on the other leg, the wheel had gone full circle, and the defeated Huns were escaping in disorder . . . The Germans went on, wild eyed, unshaven, unkempt, on foot, in stolen cars, in horse drawn vehicles, even in carts belonging to the street cleaning department. There was no attempt at military formation . . . Whereas last September they came with machine guns trained on the Romans, it was a different matter now. They were frightened. They had a clear idea of the strength of the underground movement, the power of the armed patriots and their determination to take action when and if necessary . . . A current report ran that the Germans had promised the Pope that they would not destroy anything in Rome if he would be personally responsible for the welfare of the wounded whom they might leave behind . . . By five o'clock in the afternoon the streets were almost empty of Germans; a few were still going along the Corso d'Italia . . . From one of our windows we looked down on Rome. The electric light which had been cut off was turned on abruptly, and un-curtained windows flashed out brightly like a signal of liberation to come. Then, as if on the stage, all was dark once more; except for the moonlight shining through a veil of mist. Suddenly, from the Porta Pia came a burst of wild cheering. The Allies had entered Rome . . . after that the whole town came to life. There was talk and laughter in all the streets, even in the narrowest ones; there was cheering

and the sound of clapping everywhere.[26]

(*Mother Mary St Luke*, 4 June 1944)

Another observer of these events was the journalist de Wyss:

Finally, I saw the beaten German Army retreating. There were lorries and wagons so overloaded with soldiers that they all hung around in bunches; carts with soldiers, also soldiers on horseback, peasant vehicles crammed with dead-tired men . . . and finally once soldiers passed by riding on oxen, endless rows of those going on foot. Their faces grey with fatigue, eyes popping out, mouths wide open, they limped, barefoot, dragging their rifles after them. I remember the same army entering France – contemptuous, almighty, trampling over the weaker. I remembered being thrown into a ditch by them. Now I was witnessing their defeat. My jaws clenched.[27]

The tumult and the shouting died about 1.00 a.m. and we scattered from our observation post. My own first sight of the Allies was dramatic in its simplicity. Opening a window at about six o'clock, I saw one little jeep with four American soldiers in it, making its way slowly and soundlessly along the street. No one else was about. The thing looked so solitary, yet so significant in the cool stillness of dawn. I had it all to myself for a few seconds. It was so small, yet so secure; a vignette on the page of history; a full stop at the end of the chapter of oppression and fear . . . The population of Rome seemed double what it had been; men who had been hiding for months – patriots, Italian soldiers, Allied prisoners of war who had escaped from their prison camps, young men of military age and persecuted Jews – were out and about. Bicycles appeared from their hiding places as if by magic. Rome had not seen such animation and laughter since the beginning of the War.[28]

(*Mother Mary St Luke*, 5 June 1944)

Other individuals and groups had similar experiences. Harold Tittmann notes:

Early the next morning, June 5th, our entire family went to

the spot in the nuns' garden where I had been watching the Germans the previous day, and joyfully witnessed the passage of American vehicles heading north in the pursuit of Germans. A jeep stopped briefly below us, and we shouted welcoming words in English to its occupants. Obviously surprised, one of the soldiers asked us who we were. When he learned that we were Americans, he reached to the back of the vehicle, pulled out a carton of cigarettes, a box of Hershey bars and a copy of Time magazine which he proceeded to toss over the wall in our direction. This was our first, happy contact with American soldiers. [29]

John Furman was also on the move on this historic day. He walked up to a jeep to shake hands with the driver and congratulate him on the success of the Fifth Army.

Say, you speak good English for an Italiano, he said. Perhaps because I am English, I replied, smiling. He looked at me amazed. Well, whadda ya know? Say what are you doing here anyway? I thought for a moment. It was an apt question. What was I doing here? Why was I not at home with my wife, playing with the two year old daughter I had never seen? Why were we all here? Why had the world gone mad? I was suddenly tired and in no mood to answer the philosophical questions I was ready to pose to myself. I slapped the driver on the back. Just playing a game I said, a game of hide and seek. But it is all over now. As I turned away, the driver leaned across to his mate. I heard a mutter, say, that guy's crazy. Playing hide and seek![30]

Denis Johnston, the Irish playwright, was then travelling with the British army as a BBC War Correspondent. Some days later he was in the Irish Legation.

On the neutral territory of the Irish Legation a small party of un-neutral Hibernians gathered to greet the Minister and his handsome, Rabelaisian wife . . . What was the first sign you had that we had arrived? I asked of Delia. She tossed her head of black curls, and smiled the smile that must have baffled many an Axis official. They call me your Excellency here. It is the way they have in the Diplomatic, d'ye know. Well, I was out taking a walk in the morning to see what was going on. And there was a lot of lads in uniform lying on the pavement in front of the railway station, taking a rest, d'ye know. And I thought they were Germans, until suddenly one of them sat up and said, 'Say, sister. Come and park your arse beside me'. So then I knew I was liberated.[31]

He also heard some stories of the Monsignor. 'At the Kiernans' I was told stories of the fabulous Fr O'Flaherty – long sought by the Germans for his help to Allied prisoners and refugees.'[32] Johnston and a colleague of his were also in the congregation when the Pope addressed the crowd in St Peter's Square. After the Pope's address, both felt they should celebrate the occasion.

We clasped hands and sang one of our favourite ballads for the delectation of the Roman populace – the Ould Orange Flute. It may be that this was the first time that the Ould Orange Flute has been sung on the steps of St Peter's. Its choice was a sincere tribute to the universality of the occasion. It seemed only fitting that we should sing one of our own tribal ballads in his honour, rather than something that was not ourselves.[33]

13

Critics and Admirers

The changed circumstances left the diplomats and indeed the Vatican authorities in a difficult position. Now the diplomatic representatives of the Axis powers, including Germany, Japan and Slovakia, were seeking the safe sanctuary of the Vatican accommodation. However, the Vatican authorities had no room to accommodate them until the representatives of the Allied powers moved out. The British were very conscious of the function that D'Arcy Osborne had been able to play from within the Vatican, and they were concerned that if von Weizsaecker, the German Ambassador, were to move in, he could perform a similar role for his government. Indeed, British intelligence had recommended to their Government that the German Ambassador should be not allowed inside Vatican City. The British took the view that they were not bound by the terms of the Lateran Pact as it was merely an agreement between Italy and the Holy See. It is surely one of the most ironic features of this entire episode that, by and large, the Germans had respected the terms of the Pact right throughout the War, when they must have been sorely tempted to do otherwise, whereas the British, when their turn came, tended to dismiss it. D'Arcy Osborne was in a very awkward position. He was unhappy with the view taken by his Government, but at the same time had a responsibility to represent it in negotiations with the Vatican authorities. He was conscious of the fact that the Italians and the Germans had treated the Vatican in a very proper manner by accommodating diplomats, such as himself and Tittmann, and he felt his own country should behave similarly.

Kiernan was doing his best to assist his colleagues, the German and Japanese Ambassadors, who were now under pressure. Denis Johnston observes:

> Ireland was sticking to its traditional policy of being on the side of the hunted rather than the hunter – whoever that might be . . . I must confess to finding a certain pride in Kiernan's attitude, and I did my best to help him in his undertaking.[1]

Eventually the Americans broke ranks and ordered Tittmann to move out of the Vatican leaving the British with no option but to follow suit. As they left, von Weizsaecker and Herada, the Japanese Ambassador, moved in. The German Ambassador was lucky that he made that move. On 20 July 1944, an assassination attempt on Hitler failed. It was suspected by the authorities in Berlin that von Weizsaecker was one of the conspirators. The fact that he was within the Vatican, and out of reach, probably saved his life. Whether he was opposed to Hitler or not, Kiernan certainly gave credit to his German counterpart for his work:

> All through the period of the German occupation of Rome, von Weizsaecker was a moderating influence on the military and police authorities . . . It was largely due to von Weizsaecker and a triumph of diplomacy over the horrors of war, that the German troops and the SS respected the sovereign rights and the integrity of the Vatican City state, including the buildings outside the Vatican which, being Vatican property, enjoyed extra-territorial rights.[2]

D'Arcy Osborne was now the senior diplomatic representative of the Allied countries in Rome. So the British Legation became the centre of activity in contrast to its previous existence as something of a backwater. Many of the requests coming to the Legation were from the Allied military authorities who were now in charge of Rome. D'Arcy Osborne appointed Derry as Liaison Officer, filling the role of temporary Military Attaché to the British Legation. Derry also had the role of dealing with the repatriation of those escapees whom the organisation had been supporting. A repatriation unit was established, headed by Derry, assisted by Simpson, Furman, Captain Burns and the Greek, Meletiou. They started work immediately, providing continuing funds for the escapees living in and about Rome and arranging for them to return to their units or indeed to their home countries. The person in their care who was most quickly re-united with his family was young Paul Freyberg. His father, the General, came into Rome to collect his son and a few days later they were joined by his mother.

Aside from arranging the repatriation of those for whom they had been caring over the previous months, the group turned its attention to repaying money which had been given to O'Flaherty over the years and which he, in turn, had spent on escaped Allied soldiers. They also began to make payments to individual Italians who had spent their own money directly on escapees and evaders. So the biscuit tins, which contained the records of the organisation from the time Derry became involved and had been carefully buried in the Vatican Gardens, were now dug up. His foresight in arranging a record-keeping system had proved very valuable. This screening committee headed by Derry continued to work for three years and during the course of its existence investigated more than 90,000 cases, presented 75,000 certificates of thanks signed by Field Marshal Alexander on behalf of the British Government and repaid £1 million in cash to those who had given money to O'Flaherty and his associates and others who had helped in this sort of work (in excess of €40 million in current terms). In relation to British Government funds which had been expended on military personnel from other jurisdictions, the first to repay was the Russian Government which refunded £25,000 (in excess of €1 million in current terms).

The arrival of the Allies in Rome changed the direction of Derry's work. It had a similar impact on the focus of O'Flaherty's. Sam Derry recalls a conversation between the Monsignor and the US General, Mark Clark, when the Irishman quizzed the American sharply to make sure German prisoners were well treated. The Englishman also recalls meeting the Monsignor on the day Rome was liberated.

Well my lad there is work to be done and off he went into the

City to visit some of our helpers and their relations who had suffered so much as a result of their activities on our behalf. In the evening he was back in the British Legation to see the Minister and myself with a list of requests for immediate action, some of which were not so easy to meet, considering the general chaos in Rome immediately after the liberation.[3]

Unfortunately, we do not have much detail on the Monsignor's activities in the next few months. We know, however, that he continued to help those in need of his assistance, as he always had. His situation was easier now insofar as he was not in danger of arrest and execution. Now he was helping Italians and some Austrians who had fought under the German flag. As always, he neglected himself in the interest of others. Of course he was always particularly generous with his time when he came across a fellow Irishman.

Billy Vincent is a member of the Bourn Vincent family who bought Muckross Estate in Killarney in 1910. His father presented the entire property to the nation in 1932. During the War, Billy served as a Captain in the Inniskilling Fusiliers and he was wounded at a battle on Monte Spaduro. As a result, he was transferred to a hospital in Rome in November 1944. Among the staff were a couple of Irish nurses who were friendly with the young priests and clerical students in the Irish College which was nearby. One of the priests there, Fr Seán Quinlan, was also a native of Killarney, and when he heard that Billy was in the hospital, he came to visit. 'I must tell Monsignor O'Flaherty that you are in the hospital because he would have known your father.'[4] The very next day, O'Flaherty called to the hospital and that is when they first met. At that stage, Billy was very restricted in his movement and could only walk with the help of a cane. He was delighted when O'Flaherty offered to drive him around to see the sights of Rome.

In the next few weeks, Monsignor O'Flaherty could not possibly have been kinder to me. Every two or three days he would arrive with his car at the hospital and would take me around Rome. This was an experience I shall never forget because he knew Rome absolutely backwards and had written a guidebook on all its treasures . . . He was so good to me while I was recovering in hospital; he gave me such a good education of not only the Vatican but all sorts of other treasures in Rome.[5]

In his recent recall of these events, he made no reference to the Monsignor's driving abilities. His fellow Kerryman boasted widely that he must be a great driver given the fact that his record was absolutely clear of any accident although he was driving in Rome where the worst drivers in the world were, according to him. Others took a different view and felt his accident-free record was more likely due to divine intervention. When Billy was ready to leave hospital he wanted to acknowledge his fellow Killarney man for his generosity.

I wanted to give him a present and did not know what he would like. I asked him and he said 'I would like a pair of army boots like you have, if you could get them'. I looked at his shoes and they seemed to be alright and then he lifted up his foot and there were hardly any soles on his shoes. He had been walking all over Rome during the war with really only the uppers of his shoes. I was amazed. I would never have thought he had suffered in this way, so naturally I got a pair of army boots for him and he was delighted.[6]

Derry made Alexander, the Supreme Allied Commander in Italy, aware of O'Flaherty's work. The General called on the Monsignor to express his gratitude. He proved to be of great support in succeeding months. Derry recalls the views expressed by the Monsignor at that meeting: 'His only interest was what the Allies were going to do for the Italian families who had suffered.'[7]

There were many Italian prisoners of war, mainly in South Africa, and their relatives now sought out O'Flaherty as the person most likely to be able to help. He realised that securing passage by ship or indeed by air to South Africa would be a slow process but with the intervention of Alexander, he was able to get there quickly and set up a communication system designed to locate the prisoners of war and report back to their families at home. He also flew to Israel at that time and made arrangements for many of the Jews, whom he had placed in secure locations in Rome, to be moved there. The diversion of Derry to other duties means that many of these events are not recorded. It is just like the earlier period, when we know only a fraction of what O'Flaherty achieved.

Inevitably during this time, many Fascist collaborators came to trial. Two were alleged double agents, Dr Cipolla and Aldo Zambardi, the man who had first escorted Derry to the Vatican. The Monsignor testified on their behalf. As he explained to Derry, 'They did wrong, but there is good in every man.'[8]

Before the end of the War, the Monsignor returned home to Ireland on a visit and arranged to fly back through London in order to help one Italian family. An Italian woman in Rome, who was married to a German, had asked the Monsignor to try to locate her son who was in a prisoner-of-war camp somewhere in England. She had no idea where he was. The woman wanted the Monsignor to tell her son that his father had died. O'Flaherty arranged to have one day in London and was able to use the goodwill available to him there to locate the son, who was in a camp in Chelmsford. An official government car brought O'Flaherty there. He spent his day with the young man, as he had with so many others, engaged in the role of a pastor consoling him on the death of his father.

The *London Gazette* carries announcements on behalf of the British Government, including honours which have been awarded. Inevitably, during a time of war, military personnel feature prominently. However, in the long history of the publication which dates from the middle of the seventeenth century, the issue which was published on Friday 20 April 1945 must be one of the most unusual. Among the 40 people listed were eight Catholic priests and one Catholic Brother. The entire list was headed by Monsignor O'Flaherty who was awarded a CBE. Also honoured 'for services to the forces in Italy' were Frs Borg, Galea, Madden, Buckley, Claffey, Gatt, Lenan, Treacy and Br Robert Pace, each of whom received an OBE. Mrs Henrietta Chevalier was awarded a British Empire Medal. Each recipient, including the Monsignor, was described as 'British resident in Rome'. As O'Flaherty was born before the Irish

State was established, this is a technically correct statement of his nationality. However, it is reasonably certain that the Monsignor was not made aware of this description at the time, and certainly would not have been happy with it. Right through his life, although he was entitled to a Vatican passport, it was the Irish one he used. Honoured on other occasions were the Greek Averoff, who received an OBE, and the military personnel Derry, Furman and Simpson. Typical of his modest nature, O'Flaherty arranged for his award to be made in a simple ceremony in the British Embassy in Rome. Shortly after that he was also awarded the US Medal of Freedom with Silver Palm (a very rare award for a non-American civilian), the citation reading:

> For exceptionally meritorious conduct in the performance of outstanding services to the Government of the United States in Italy between March of 1912 and June of 1944. His untiring energy and efforts, often at the risk of his own life, and his unfailing devotion to the cause of freedom were exemplified in the concrete aid given to so many prisoners-of-war.[9]

Subsequently, the President of Italy, on behalf of the Government, awarded the Monsignor a silver medal for military valour with an accompanying pension.

> During the occupation of Rome, despite the persistent surveillance by the enemy, he spent himself courageously to assist and conceal numerous Allied prisoners-of-war and groups of patriots. With tireless energy, and paying no heed to the grave risks to which he continually exposed himself – both in his home (which he made into his operational base) and in the quarters of other resistance organisations, he distinguished himself by his brave and consistent combative action, in such ways as to give clear, shining example both of valour and of service. Singled out and relentlessly sought by the enemy, he still managed to achieve many and dangerous missions of war calmly facing the peril to his life, in order to practice at all times his high dedication to humanity and the cause of liberty.[10]

The Monsignor never bothered to collect the pension. As Sam Derry was to remark many years later, O'Flaherty 'wanted nothing for himself'.[11]

D'Arcy Osborne was anxious that recognition would be given to the work of Mrs Kiernan (Delia Murphy) and indeed Mrs Kiernan's name was suggested for a decoration. However there were obvious difficulties. A British Government honour to the wife of an Ambassador from a neutral country for activities which were far from impartial could raise questions. By way of compromise, D'Arcy Osborne gave her a vase which she treasured greatly. Wherever her husband's postings brought her for the rest of her life, including Australia and North America, the vase went with her.

The ending of the War meant that O'Flaherty could resume his love affair with the golf course. Through playing golf on the course near Ciampino he became aware of a very neglected village full of people gravely stricken by poverty, who were worshipping at a tiny, half ruined church. He immediately took up the challenge and looked after this congregation for the next twelve years. His attention was to both religious and pastoral matters. He made practical arrangements, including ensuring that his contacts in Rome were used to the best advantage in order to supply this congregation with food and the necessities of life. The church was tiny, big enough only for the altar, the celebrant and the altar server. The congregation used to assemble outside. Among the congregation one Sunday, on a visit from Ireland, was his sister, Bride Sheehan. Over the years, she had endeavoured many times to give her brother money, to ensure that he had some of the comforts of life. She thought this was her opportunity and so she placed a big donation on the collection plate. Little did she realise that the collection plate, including the contribution from the locals and from O'Flaherty's friends who attended Mass there, was disbursed among the poor immediately after Mass every Sunday. When people whom he had helped contacted him from abroad as to see how they could return the favour, he invariably asked for them to send clothes to help this congregation. Regularly, parcels arrived from some of the major shops in places like London and New York and soon members of the congregation were as well dressed as any in the general area of Rome.

The Kiernans were home on holidays during August 1946. Monsignor O'Flaherty was also in Ireland at that time. All three were invited to a lunch by a Fr Campion who was then a priest stationed in Kill, County Kildare. Also invited was the young Dublin singer, Veronica Dunne, whom the priest had recognised as having exceptional talent. She came along with her mother. Fr Campion was anxious that Delia Murphy would hear Veronica singing, which she did during the course of the afternoon. All the company agreed that further training was the next appropriate step to take but the question arose as to where. At that stage, most of the major capitals in Europe had been virtually destroyed, so Rome seemed an obvious choice. Monsignor O'Flaherty offered to help and subsequently went out to where the family lived on the Howth Road and met Veronica's father. It was agreed that Veronica would undertake further training in Rome and the Monsignor would act as a guardian. Fr Campion was a renowned host but Veronica recollects that Monsignor O'Flaherty did not really eat that much. With the scarcities that applied in Rome and his generosity to other people, he had neglected himself and now found that the rich food available at the lunch did not suit him.

In September 1946 Veronica flew out to Rome, then a twelve-hour journey including various stops. The Monsignor was there to meet her and immediately made clear what was expected: 'See that plane, there. If I see you with any of those Italian men you will be going straight back.'[12] Her first encounter with Roman manhood was interesting. O'Flaherty drove into the city from the airport but had to stop at a Post Office to do some business. Meanwhile Veronica sitting in the vehicle found herself surrounded by some Italian men who were hissing at her, but when the Monsignor returned, he had a ready explanation. 'They think you are my mistress.'[13] Indeed, that may have been the explanation. An alternative possibility was that the Monsignor was trying to hide from her that anti-clericalism was not uncommon in Rome at that time.

He then brought her to a convent where she stayed for a few months. Subsequently he found suitable accommodation for her with a family. She remembers going around the Eternal City with him. 'They treated him like a God, not just the Romans but the American, British and French soldiers also.'[14] He brought her to all the receptions and got her tickets for the various big events. The first one was a dinner for one of the senior Allied generals, which was held in a major hotel in the city about ten days after she arrived, at which an eight-course dinner was served. She found herself sitting away from the top table beside a very charming and good-looking South African major. He asked her did she like the Roman ice cream. When she explained that she had not tasted any yet, he offered to bring her out for some after the meal. So when the final course was finished she went to seek the Monsignor's permission. She noticed very early on in her dealings with the Monsignor that, if he got concerned or indeed angry about anything, his eyes seemed to widen, magnified by the glasses he usually wore. On this occasion his eyes widened but also he scratched his head in curiosity as he could not understand why she needed ice cream after an eight-course dinner. Eventually, he gave permission with the instruction that she be back in plenty of time so that he could leave her home and return to the Vatican before eleven o'clock. Unfortunately, she was late back, not arriving to the hotel until about a quarter to eleven.

> 'Do you realise now I will be late back to the Vatican and I will have to climb over a big wall in order to get home.' 'Sure Monsignor', she replied, 'with your long legs, you will be well able to do that.'[15]

Veronica stayed in Rome for nearly four years and they established a wonderful relationship. The arrangement was that she would have lunch with him every Friday and explain what she had been doing. She also might get a phone call every now and again just to check up on her. She quickly found that the Monsignor had so many friends around Rome, particularly the Irish priests, that in fact she had scores of guardians rather than one. She recalls one Friday calling to his home and finding him very sad. It seems that one of the Fascists who was to be executed had asked him to be present and this whole episode disturbed him greatly.

As with others, he did not talk to her about what he had done during the War. She was aware, however, through meeting so many people who knew him, and held him in such high regard, that he had achieved great things. She also knew that he was still working both for German and Italians who were in trouble with the Allied authorities and for refugees living in various locations around Rome. Each Saturday, he delivered food and provisions to these people. All these were paid for by the Pope and O'Flaherty regularly told her that the Pope had always been a great support to him.

Gallagher, an Irish journalist, records a cloud over O'Flaherty's career after the War. As we have already seen, Vatican officialdom at that stage was very much Italian-dominated and he was seen as an outsider. Indeed, it was another 40 years or so before another Irishman secured a similarly high position in the Vatican Curia, the late Archbishop of Dublin, Dermot Ryan. Aside from that of course many working in the Vatican would have been genuinely worried that his activities, if discovered, would have been hugely embarrassing and indeed could have compromised the Pope's policy of neutrality. Apart from any Italians who may have resented him, he had at least one other very definite critic. On 28 November 1944, MacWhite of the Irish Legation in Rome reports back to Dublin:

> Monsignor O'Flaherty of the Holy Office became renowned during the War as a protector and Guardian of British War Prisoners who had found their way to Rome from Prison Camps. He boasted that considerable sums of money were placed at his disposal for the purpose by Prince Doria who was appointed Mayor of Rome by the Allies for his generosity. O'Flaherty's activities got known to the Germans who probably made a protest to the Vatican and he was confined to quarters for several months. I have also heard it stated that he acted as an agent for the British Minister to the Holy See in finding shelter, providing identity cards and in other ways aiding British agents and prisoners of war. As a recompense for these services he was recently permitted to go by air to South Africa to visit a diocese to which he is supposed to be attached. On the way, he was conducted to the pyramids and

other show places – all presumably at the cost of the British Government.[16]

His report some months later in January 1945 is even stronger.

In three of last Sunday's papers one could read how an Irish Monsignor deceived the SS by pretending to be a coalman. It has all the appearances of having been contributed by the person concerned who has a mania for publicity. How far it is true, I cannot say, but the implications are that he was the agent of the British Minister to the Holy See, if not one of his spies. It will hardly get him sympathy in the Holy Office.[17]

The allegations contained in these two reports vary from the trivial to the serious. It is hardly likely that the Monsignor, who was so understated about his work, went to the bother of placing this report in the newspapers. O'Flaherty wrote no account of his activities himself. He gave just one interview, to the Irish journalist J. P. Gallagher, in 1958. Gallagher recounts that it took him six days to persuade O'Flaherty to give the interview. The Duchess of Sermoneta had similar experiences of O'Flaherty:

A large volume could be filled with stories of thrilling adventures in which his life was constantly in danger. I know how he gave away practically all the clothes he possessed except those he stood up in, and that night after night, he slept on the floor so that an exhausted man could rest in his bed, but the trouble is that he will not let me write about his own activities and persists in telling me only what other people did. He has a special admiration for the courage of the Roman women who never failed to help him in his work. He said there were many, rich or poor, that he could always count on.[18]

These are not the actions of a publicity seeker. Even in the highly unlikely event that he did place this report in the papers, it is hardly a serious charge. It is of course true to say that he spent a lot of his time and energy in helping escapees. In doing this however, he was not acting as an agent for the British Minister to the Holy See. He was merely following the dictates of his conscience. The suggestion that the trip to South Africa was a recompense for helping British escapees is ill-founded. As we know, this was O'Flaherty taking advantage of an offer of help to continue his work. The most serious charge however is the implication that he might have been a spy. There is no doubt that part of Derry's work with the organisation related to gathering information and passing it on to the Allies as they approached Rome. There is no evidence anywhere that O'Flaherty was involved in this work, although he was aware of it. Indeed D'Arcy Osborne was aware that such a charge might arise, and in securing the services of a British officer when he did, he was insulating the Monsignor against future criticism. Aside from that, if Derry had needed assistance in this aspect of his work, he had available to him hundreds of trained military personnel. The suggestion that he would ignore those possibilities and choose a priest, who was well known in Rome and who was on the run from the authorities, to do this work, does not stand up to any serious examination. Of course, MacWhite had very justifiable reasons to be concerned regarding the Monsignor's activities. With his military training it was easy for him to foresee what might happen to O'Flaherty if he were caught. Moreover, there could have been serious implications, in that eventuality, for some of the Irish living in Rome for whose welfare the diplomat felt a keen sense of responsibility.

Veronica Dunne recalls the Monsignor being quite disillusioned with the politics he experienced in the Vatican. On more than one occasion, he said to her that politics there were worse than elsewhere. She also discerned a serious amount of jealousy among some in the Vatican arising from his fame and popularity around Rome. The very welcome contrast between the straight-talking Veronica and some of those he was dealing with on a daily basis surely contributed to the wonderful friendship that grew up between them. Her view of him is very clear. She remembers his sense of humour. Giving her a ticket for a papal audience one day, he warned her, 'Watch out for the nuns, they will jump all over you.[19] Her recollection is that he was right. Aside from his sense of humour, she particularly remembers his care for her and indeed everyone else. 'He was a gentle gentle man, he really was . . . a very clever and a very lovable man . . . a great, great man.'[20]

It has been suggested, from time to time, that O'Flaherty might have been happier in the role of an Irish parish priest. His nephew thinks there is a strong possibility that this is true and that deep-down his uncle might have liked to have been an Irish parish priest dealing with more straightforward people than those he was meeting in the Vatican. He also recalls him dismissing the possibility in a jocose fashion. One time when the Monsignor was at home on holidays, all the family were invited to lunch by Fr Tim O'Sullivan who was then the parish priest on Valentia Island, and a renowned host. A big spread was laid on for lunch with a roast as the main feature. Fr Tim made a great ceremony of carving this roast. The Monsignor, on the way home after the visit, said rather ruefully, 'I could never have been a Parish Priest in Ireland because I cannot carve.'[21]

Danny O'Connor of Cahersiveen also has very fond memories of the Monsignor. They first came in contact when O'Flaherty returned home on holidays from Rome and Danny was assigned to serve Mass for him. To the altar boys of that era, a returning senior cleric usually generated mixed emotions. There was awe at the arrival of this important person which was tempered somewhat by the possibility that he might be a good tipper. Indeed the Monsignor did not disappoint on that front. In relation to the awe it was another matter: 'I suppose I was a bit afraid of him. I soon realised there was no need. He was a very gentle, quiet man.'[20] He recalls the Monsignor as having no airs and graces and being a careful, but not ostentatious dresser, wearing a simple soutane with the barest piece of purple under the Roman collar indicating his status as a Monsignor. Indeed, this lack of 'show' disappointed the Monsignor's brother, Jim. He would have preferred Hugh to wear the full purple stock to indicate his elevated status within the Church, and chided him regularly for dressing so conservatively.

14

An Unsung Hero

Early in 1953, Pope Pius XII made Monsignor O'Flaherty a Domestic Prelate which is an honour conferred on priests who have undertaken outstanding work. Six years later he was appointed Head Notary of the Holy Office and from then on, all the documents and decrees published by this, the oldest of the Vatican's Congregations, carried his name. Meanwhile his friendship with Ottaviani, the Head of the Holy Office continued. Ottaviani had no sight in one eye and very limited sight in the other. Frequently, he and the Monsignor sat down to recite their breviary together with the Irishman reading sections and Ottaviani reciting, from memory, other pieces. O'Flaherty made regular visits home, always trying to avail of an opportunity to visit Croke Park if Kerry had made it to the later stages of the All-Ireland Championship. Because he took his holidays in August, he was rarely home for a Final but usually managed to attend semi-finals. He was so interested in the fortunes of Kerry that Cardinal Ottaviani became engrossed in keeping up to date as to how they were doing although he certainly had never been in Kerry and, almost certainly, had never seen a Gaelic football match. Fr Seán Quinlan recalls meeting O'Flaherty one day in Rome when the Monsignor told him Ottaviani had been sick in bed for a week. To Quinlan's amusement Monsignor O'Flaherty ascribed the illness of the stern and austere Cardinal to the fact that Kerry had recently been knocked out of the Championship.

While undoubtedly his visits home were enjoyable, another series of calls which he made were more interesting. Kappler, the

Gestapo Chief, had been arrested and found guilty of war crimes, particularly arising out of the massacre in the Ardeatine Caves. He was sentenced to life imprisonment and placed in a prison at Gaeta half way between Rome and Naples. He had only one visitor during his period there, a monthly caller, the Irish Monsignor. Also, they exchanged letters regularly. These contacts were not universally admired. The Communist newspaper *Avanti* in its issue of 11 October 1951, comments:

> We learn . . . that an eminent member of the curia has taken much to heart the fate of Kappler, we cannot be exact if this is because of a charitable Christian Heart or is an assignment for higher hierarchies. It is of course the famous Irish Monsignor Ugo O'Flaherty . . . he has become Kappler's number one protector. It turns out that the Monsignor is moving heaven and earth to free the 'executioner of Rome' from his imprisonment . . .[1]

By this time MacWhite had retired from his post. Obviously his concern with regard to O'Flaherty's activities survived in the Embassy after his departure and were shared by at least one other official there who took the trouble to refer this newspaper article back to the Dublin authorities for their attention. As it happens, there is no evidence that the Monsignor was involved in any work to free Kappler. His concerns were more pastoral. The Monsignor baptised Kappler into the Catholic faith some years later.

Fr Leonard Boyle went to work in the Dominican University in Rome in 1955. He used to buy a daily paper at a news-stand on the edge of St Peter's Square. Many years later he recalled a conversation with the newspaper seller:

> One day the man said to me 'what nationality are you'. I said I was Irish and he said 'did you know Hugh O'Flaherty'. I said 'yes I did, just casually', and he said 'there is the greatest man I have ever met'. I said, 'how did you know him'. He said 'I ran this store during the War and this was Hugh O'Flaherty's post box. He would give me letters and I would do the runner for him and I was in my teens at the time.'[2]

While his countryman, MacWhite, was one of a number who clearly were not very impressed with the Monsignor's activities, O'Flaherty made a far more favourable impression on others. Tittmann describes the various people he and his family got to know in Rome:

> One of our favourites among the clergy was a lively Irishman, Monsignor Hugh O'Flaherty of the Supreme Sacred Congregation of the Holy Office. His activities in finding safe hiding places, both inside the Vatican and elsewhere, for Allied escaped prisoners-of-war and other refugees from the Germans, made him literally famous. He lived practically next door to us, just outside the Vatican walls, on the Via Teutonica; he often came into Santa Marta on business and delighted us with his countless amusing stories.[3]

Tittmann's eldest son, also called Harold, recalls that 'O'Flaherty came to dinner with us on several occasions in Santa Marta. I vividly recall his imposing presence (he was a very tall man) and his remarkable sense of humour.'[4]

Indeed it is noticeable that the Monsignor got on well with young people generally, including the Kiernan family, and those whom he met in Cahersiveen when on holidays. It was not uncommon in those days for people living near the sea to be quite ignorant of how to swim. He devoted much of the time he spent at home on holidays teaching young people in the locality this very important skill.

In his account of the battle for Rome the historian Raleigh Trevelyan notes:

> The originator of the Rome Organisation was an Irish Monsignor from Killarney, Fr Hugh O'Flaherty, a magnetic character, fanatically keen on golf, tall, a considerable joker, with a thick brogue and blue eyes behind round steel-rimmed spectacles – a scarlet pimpernel maybe, but no Baroness Orczy hero in appearance, in spite of cloak, sash and wide rimmed black hat.[5]

John Furman held him in great respect, not only for his work but for another interesting facet of his character:

> Coupled with his work in the Holy Office of the Vatican, he
> made sufficient time to organise billets for refugees and
> hiding-places for aristocrats, Jews and anti-Fascists who were
> in danger. He found them clothes and food. Those who
> deserved it felt the lash of his tongue. Those who needed it
> received the comfort of his sympathy. Through the six
> months of German occupation while I was in almost daily
> contact with him, he never once tried to 'sell' me religion,
> another trait for which I held him in deep respect. I did not
> look on him as a priest but as a very good friend who made
> other people's troubles his own.[6]

In early 1960 the Church authorities had discussed with
O'Flaherty the possibility of appointing him as Papal Nuncio to
Tanzania but unfortunately by the middle of the year his health
began to fail him and he suffered his first stroke. He spent several
weeks in the hospital in Rome before retiring officially from his
post in September of that year. He returned to live in Cahersiveen,
County Kerry, with his sister Bride Sheehan in that year, though
occasionally he left to do some technical, legal and canonical work
for the Diocese of Los Angeles. While he was limited to some
extent by the effects of the stroke, he was anxious to keep working
at all times. By the time he returned to live in Cahersiveen, Danny
O'Connor, his former altar boy, was now working in Mrs Sheehan's
shop. Their friendship developed further and Danny began to gain
a fuller picture of the Monsignor's character, remembering him as
'a man of strong character and determination who was at the same
time very gentle and hated to see even animals hurt.'[7]

Danny also remembers the Monsignor's interest in gadgetry
and recollects gifts of an electric razor (a Remington) and the first
transistor radio he had ever seen. As he was somewhat hampered
by the effects of his stroke, any time the Monsignor wanted to go
on a long journey, Danny drove him. They spent many hours
together. The Monsignor never spoke about events in Rome during
the War. In his chats with Danny the topics were, invariably, the
fortunes of the local and county football teams and the activities of

the various characters in the town. Not only did O'Flaherty love football matches but the entire experience before and afterwards, mixing with the crowd, and meeting people he knew, was always a joy to him. He loved the trips to Dublin for matches in Croke Park, meeting people on the train or in the station, meeting others on O'Connell Street or in the Gresham Hotel. It was only in later years, and from others, that Danny began to learn the nature of the work the Monsignor had been involved in while he was living in Rome. For example, he recalls Mrs Sheehan telling him that on a holiday in Rome when the Monsignor was still there she was recognised by a family of Jewish people whom he had helped. They brought her into the jewellery shop which they owned and insisted on presenting her with a piece of her choice.

The producers of the BBC TV programme *This is Your Life* decided in late 1962 to make a programme in tribute to the Monsignor. However, by this stage his health was failing and it was clear that it would be very inadvisable for him to travel over to London. As a result they altered the focus of the programme and decided to feature Sam Derry. He recalls that in February 1963:

> I was manoeuvred into a London Television Studio, the unwitting subject of *This is your Life*. Before an audience of former POWs, colleagues from the British organisation in Rome came forth to share old memories. A white-haired Monsignor O'Flaherty appeared on film, sending greetings from Ireland in a halting, quavering voice, because (it was explained) doctors warned him not to travel.[8]

In his contribution the Monsignor recalled those difficult times:

> These were dark days and I shall always remember the difficulties we had in trying to keep one step ahead of the Gestapo. Sam, when you came to Rome you arrived at the right moment. Events were getting difficult for me. I needed a British Officer with some authority and, when I mentioned your name and when he saw you, the British Minister said to me you were the right man.[9]

A number of the leaders of the organisation were interviewed during the programme including John Furman and Bill Simpson. Then Norman Anderson was brought on to tell his story of his appendectomy. In keeping with the focus of the programme the presenter, the renowned Irish broadcaster Eamonn Andrews, conducted the interview with Anderson as though Sam Derry were the organiser of this entire escapade. This however was too much for the honourable Englishman and when Anderson attempted to thank him, Derry can clearly be heard in the recording, quietly but firmly, placing credit where it was due, that is with Monsignor O'Flaherty. Even though the programme was being broadcast almost twenty years after these events, it is interesting to note that the presenter felt it was imprudent to mention the embassy from which the car was supplied and so used the phrase:

> A car was borrowed from a neutral embassy which we won't name.[10]

As the programme came towards its end, Andrews advised Sam Derry and the audience,

> We have time enough for one more guest and this is the man whose advice you relied on during those strenuous months in Rome . . . not on film this time but here in the flesh.[11]

Sam Derry remembers:

> Suddenly Monsignor appeared and slowly walked on stage. Blinking in the limelight he grinned and threw his arms around me. We both wept for joy. That was our last time together.[12]

This must have been an emotional gathering for many in the audience, as well as for Derry and O'Flaherty. The vast majority of those who had been helped by the organisation never had the opportunity to meet either Derry or O'Flaherty. Derry was incarcerated in the Vatican and O'Flaherty was lying low for a lot of the time. Those being helped outside Rome had no chance of meeting either of them and only a fraction of those within Rome would have had the opportunity. As a consequence many in the audience now were able to express in person their gratitude to those who had assisted them.

Danny O'Connor recalls driving the Monsignor to Cork for the flight to London. He was very ill at that time but was quite determined that he would join with his friends for one last time. He died on 30 October 1963 and his funeral Mass was celebrated in the Daniel O'Connell Memorial Church the following Sunday. The President, Éamon de Valera, was represented by his ADC, Lieutenant Colonel O'Reilly. The British Military Attaché attended and there were messages of sympathy and wreaths from many of his associates located all over the world. His death was reported in a wide range of national and international newspapers. An obituary notice appeared in the Mungret College Journal written by his friend, the Jesuit Fr Francis Joy.

> Hugh O'Flaherty was above all a generous honest-to-God Irishman without guile. His big heart was open to any and every distress and he was lavish in his efforts to assuage suffering in any form, a facet of his character which made him an easy target for any hard luck story. His expenditure on charity must have been immense and his motto always was *'cast your bread upon the waters'* . . . his life was always ordered to using his powers in fair-weather or foul for the glory of God. Can any of us hope to achieve more?[13]

Around the time of the fiftieth anniversary of the Liberation of Rome, family and friends arranged for a grove of trees to be planted in memory of the Monsignor at the National Park in Killarney in 1994. To mark the occasion the Irish poet, Brendan Kennelly, wrote:

> There is a tree called freedom and it grows
> Somewhere in the hearts of men,
> Rain falls, ice freezes, wind blows,
> The tree shivers, steadies itself again,
> Steadies itself like Hugh O'Flaherty's hand,
> Guiding trapped and hunted people, day and night,
> To what all hearts love and understand,
> The tree of freedom upright in the light.

> Mediterranean Palm, Italian Cypress, Holm Oak, Stone Pine;
> A peaceful grove in honour of that man,
> Commemorates all who struggled to be free,

The hurried world is a slave of time,
Wise men are victims of their shrewdest plans.

Pause, stranger. Ponder Hugh O'Flaherty's tree.

Frank Lewis, in his *Saturday Supplement* programme for Radio Kerry, covered the event. Sam Derry was one of those invited to attend but unfortunately ill health prevented him. For the programme, he was interviewed on the telephone. He recounted many of the episodes in O'Flaherty's life during the War. During the course of the interview it became clear that, in preparation, he had made some notes which he would like to share with the listeners. Clearly the Englishman, who died two years later, was taking this opportunity to pay one last tribute to his colleague:

> Various things I shall always remember him for, his courage, his faith in God and people, his kindness, his devotion and his indifference to personal comfort as far as he himself was concerned. Once he had made up his mind what was right, the determination to do all in his power despite all obstacles to see the matter through to the end, driving himself both physically and mentally beyond the normal limits. His strict code of self discipline, never relaxing or neglecting the duties of his chosen profession. What had to be done, had to be done that day, and must not be left until the next day. However tired we might be after walking many many miles around Rome visiting and transporting chaps to billets, we would return to his bed study which we shared and he would say, you will have to excuse me but I have work to do. I would sleep on the settee while he would work at his desk until the early hours. Another point was his ability to see the best in people, even the vilest creatures who were capable of terrible deeds, he would feel there must be some good in them somewhere. He was quite incapable of feeling spite or a wish for revenge.[14]

The British authorities described the activities of the escape organisation in their archives as 'the British Organisation in Rome for assisting Allied escaped prisoners-of-war, 1944'. During that period there were indeed a number of British officers actively involved, as we have seen. It is notable that these men who were involved in working with O'Flaherty in their own accounts of these times do not use the term 'British Organisation'. Sam Derry's book is entitled *The Rome Escape Line*, Bill Simpson's is *A Vatican Lifeline* and, similarly, John Furman wrote a book entitled *Be Not Fearful*. The reality is that the organisation operated at two levels. On the one hand O'Flaherty, with the involvement of the British army personnel and his other colleagues, was looking after the welfare of escaped prisoners of war and other Allied Service personnel who were hiding in or around Rome. On the other hand, the Monsignor and his friends and colleagues were looking after civilians who for one reason or another were hiding from the Nazis and Fascists.

In relation to the former group, Derry set up a very detailed administrative structure. He was conscious of the fact that he was expending official government money, mainly British, on these people and he would be asked to account for it in due course. Financial support was being given to those who were housing these service personnel in order to feed and clothe them. Considerable sums of money were being expended as we have seen. Aside from Derry's records, we know a lot about these events because of the war memoirs written by various people. At the time of the Liberation of Rome, the organisation was catering for 3,925 escapees. Of these, 1,695 were British, 896 South African, 429 Russian, 425 Greek, 185 American and the remaining 300 or so from 20 different other countries including 28 citizens of what was then the Irish Free State. Over and above that there were others, numbering many hundreds, whom the organisation had assisted to escape back to Allied Lines or neutral countries. Derry was able to arrange for many of those who were on the run to be picked up off the Adriatic coast by ships. Hundreds of others managed to make their way back to neutral Switzerland through the help of Ristic Cedomir and his colleagues.

As regards the activities on behalf of civilians not nearly as much is known. O'Flaherty was placing these in Vatican property, in religious houses and convents, and indeed in private houses. He had financial resources available to him by way of donations, as we have seen, so it was not necessary to keep ongoing accounts. In any event, ongoing financial support was not that necessary as those who hosted these evaders were willing and able, for the most part, to provide for them. Almost all of the civilians he assisted were Italians and many inevitably were Jewish. The Jewish people in Rome had their own welfare organisation, DELASEM. By the autumn of 1943, in fact, a Capuchin monk, Fr Marie-Benoît, was its President. The monk was modest about his election to this position: 'I was the only committee member who was sufficiently unknown in the city to be able to go about freely – to the police, to the embassies, to the various Government offices. It was a case of Marie-Benoît, or no one.'[15] The Capuchin had come to Rome from Nice where he had previously befriended the Jews. Initially his work was in trying to secure accommodation in Italy for Jews who were leaving Nice for fear of being captured. In September 1943, he extended this work to Italian and Roman Jews and their needs. Of course, he was not nearly as well known in Rome as O'Flaherty and so while the majority of Jews seeking help would have gone to DELASEM, there is no doubt that many went to O'Flaherty. As we have seen, there were about 5,000 Jewish people hidden on papal property either in the Vatican or in the extra-territorial convents and religious houses. It is reasonable to assume that O'Flaherty was involved in ensuring the safety of hundreds if not thousands of these.

For example, Hugh O'Flaherty (his nephew) received a letter in 1995 from Sr Noreen Dennehy, a missionary Franciscan Sister, enclosing in turn a letter she had sent on to a Jewish organisation which was researching these events:

> I am very happy to tell you that I, personally, worked with Monsignor O'Flaherty in Rome during the tragic war years when he risked his life in order to help the Jews in Rome. Time after time, Monsignor came to our Franciscan Generalate, located at that time in the Via Nicola Fabrizio on the Gianiculum. He often asked us to house the persecuted Jews. Since we had a very large Generalate, we were able to accommodate as many as fourteen or fifteen at any one time. Our Superior General Mother Mary Benignus and her

assistant Mother Mary Marcarius who have both since died were very much in sympathy with the Monsignor's efforts in his noble works. It was he who gave impetus to the work: he was tireless in his efforts to help lessen the suffering of the Jewish people. He helped many people to escape hardship and inevitable death.[16]

Another similar situation arose in relation to an English-born nun, Sr Maria Antoniazzi. She became a Notre Dame Sister shortly before the Second World War started. The Order sent her to a poor part of Rome when the War broke out and, with support from Monsignor O'Flaherty, her convent became one of the safe houses in the city in which he located many Jewish children. As well as looking after their welfare when they were with her, she provided false papers for the children so that they could be smuggled out. She has been recognised by the Jewish authorities for her work arising out of testimony provided by the Jacobi family, one of the many whom she helped. In a letter to an Italian newspaper in April 1986, Ines Gistron recalls:

> Monsignor O'Flaherty placed me and my Jewish friend in a *pensione* run by Canadian Nuns at Monteverde (Rome). We were given false IDs. We lived with elderly women and young ladies, completely separated from the nuns in the cloisters. After the Nazis began searching for Jews, the *pensione* was so filled that the Holy Father ordered the cloistered areas to be opened in order to provide for more refugees.[17]

We will never know how many civilians were helped by the organisation but Bill Simpson, the Monsignor's close associate, estimates it to be about 2,000.

All in all, the Monsignor and those whom he recruited and inspired ensured the safety of more than 6,500 people. In anyone's terms this represents a great achievement and is evidence of the wide range of talents which he possessed and of great leadership qualities. It must be emphasised that all the members of the organisation which he established were volunteers, including the British. He assembled a very disparate group including many of his clerical friends – most of whom were Irish, Maltese or New

Zealanders – British servicemen, and ordinary Italian men and women very aptly described in Bill Simpson's dedication to his book as those who 'beyond rational explanation rose during the Nazi occupation from submission to heroism without leaving home.'[18]

Each of those who was helping O'Flaherty knew quite clearly the risks they were taking. At the early stages imprisonment was a certainty and as time went on the Germans made it clear that execution would follow for any of those who were caught. Of course, all played their part but O'Flaherty is due great credit for his achievements. In relation to the organisation as a whole, O'Flaherty's closest collaborator – Sam Derry – is in no doubt as to the crucial role played by the Monsignor. In the foreword to Derry's book *The Rome Escape Line*, published in 1960, he comments:

> This book has been written unbeknown to Monsignor Hugh O'Flaherty, CBE: one of the finest men it has been my privilege ever to meet. Had it not been for this gallant gentleman, there would have been no Rome Escape Organisation. [19]

In this context, it is quite surprising that there has been no official recognition of his humanitarian contribution by the civil authorities in Ireland at any level whereas, by contrast, half a dozen governments across the world honoured his achievements. While the Irish Government does not operate an honours system like many others do, there are of course options open to it if it wishes to pay tribute to an outstanding citizen. Much has been written in recent years about the fact that those who helped in any way in the British war effort tended to be ignored subsequently by 'official' Ireland. For example, the historian and broadcaster, Cathal O'Shannon, returned to Ireland after the War, having served in the RAF. He recollects that he was forbidden to wear his uniform by Irish regulation at that time. Quite understandably, he contrasts this unfavourably with the fact that a number of prominent Nazis came to live here during the decades after the War and were well received at all levels of society. Included among these were: Otto Skorzeny, who led the rescue of Mussolini from captivity and was frequently described as Hitler's favourite soldier; Andrija Artukovic who as Nazi Minister for the Interior in Croatia oversaw the extermination of approximately one million people; and one Peter Menten who personally supervised the killing of hundreds of peasants, including children, in the Ukraine. It was not until Menten, having served ten years in prison for his war crimes, announced in 1985 that he was returning to live in Ireland that the authorities finally put a stop to this sad episode.

Monsignor O'Flaherty's reputation undoubtedly suffered from the official disapproval of those who were involved with the British forces. Another definite reason for this lack of recognition lies within O'Flaherty himself. Not only was he a self-effacing man by nature, but it is clear that he did not consider his wartime work out of the ordinary. Sadly, it seems likely that the former factor was the predominant one in this lack of celebration of his outstanding achievements.

In preparation for the Holy Year of 1950 the Monsignor and Bishop John Smit wrote a guidebook to Rome entitled *O Roma Felix*. The book is an amazing amalgam of geography, history, culture and archaeology and, as such, is a very scholarly work and far richer in its content than the average guide book. No reference, of course, is made to the Monsignor's wartime activities or indeed that period in the history of Italy, with one exception: the authors refer to the bronze statue in the centre of Rome of Marcus Aurelius which is the only work of its kind surviving from Imperial times. During the War, the statue was covered to protect it from the effects of bombing and the saying developed in Rome:

Quando Marco torna alla luce,
Non trova piu né Re né Duce.

Which they translate to mean more or less,

When Marcus again returns to the light,
He will find both King and Duce in flight.

Which is of course what came to pass.

O'Flaherty was proud of this book and his nephew recalls 'he would boast about it as the best guidebook in Rome in contrast to his reticence in other directions.'[20] This outstanding book was produced by the Monsignor and his colleague to benefit pilgrims and so he obviously felt it was reasonable to boast about it. By contrast, his work for those who were on the run from the authorities was merely fulfilling his responsibilities. As a Catholic priest he was preaching the word of God and it was his duty to practise it. Clearly, that is how he viewed his work for escapees and evaders. The rest of us, however, must conclude that he fulfilled his mission with extraordinary conviction, ingenuity, courage and compassion for his fellow man. Indeed this was a great and good man.

References

Chapter 1

1.   Aidan O'Hara, *I'll live till I die: The story of Delia Murphy*, p. 53.
2.   *Ibid.* p. 52.
3.   *Ibid.* p. 53
4.   *Ibid.* p. 95.
5.   National Archives, Department of Foreign Affairs papers.
6.   *Ibid.*
7.   *Ibid.*

Chapter 2

1.   O'Flaherty family archives.
2.   *Ibid.*
3.   *Ibid.*
4.   *Ibid.*
5.   *Ibid.*
6.   *Ibid.*
7.   *Ibid.*
8.   *Ibid.*
9.   *Ibid.*
10.   *Ibid.*
11.   *Ibid.*
12.   Vittoria Sermoneta, *Sparkle Distant Worlds*, p. 261.
13.   The National Archives (UK), War Office papers.
14.   National Archives, Department of Foreign Affairs papers.
15.   *Ibid.*

16. MacWhite Archives: a letter to the Department of Foreign Affairs which most probably was never sent.
17. Sam Derry, *The Rome Escape Line* p.39.
18. J. P. Gallagher, *The Scarlet Pimpernel of the Vatican*, pp. 30–1.

Chapter 3

1. John Keegan, *The Second World War*, p. 288.
2. MacWhite Archives, a letter to the Department of Foreign Affairs.
3. *Ibid.*
4. T. J. Kiernan, *Pope Pius XII*, p. 41.
5. R. Katz, *Fatal Silence*, p. 23.
6. MacWhite Archives, a coded cablegram to Department of Foreign Affairs.
7. *Ibid.*
8. Mother Mary St Luke, *Inside Rome with the Germans*, p. 2.
9. Ibid. pp. 2–3.
10. *Ibid.* p. 4–6.
11. Kiernan, op. cit., pp. 43–4.
12. Katz, op. cit., p. 43.
13. MacWhite Archives, a coded cablegram to Department of Foreign Affairs.
14. St Luke, op. cit., pp. 8–9.
15. *Ibid.* p. 10.
16. *Ibid.* p. 10.
17. Excerpt from D'Arcy Osborne's diary, cited in Chadwick, Owen, *Britain and the Vatican during the Second World War*, p. 168.
18. Gallagher, op. cit., p. 32.
19. *Ibid.* p. 35.

Chapter 4

1. Sam Derry with David MacDonald, 'Vatican Pimpernel', *Reader's Digest*, November 1975.
2. Sr Noreen Dennehy interviewed by Maurice O'Keeffe in January 2004; CD no. 65 in his Irish Life and Lore, Kerry Collection.
3. Gallagher, op. cit. p. 57.
4. *Ibid.* p. 62.
5. St Luke, op. cit., p. 26.

6.   *Ibid.* p.27.
7.   *Ibid.* pp. 28–9.
8.   *Ibid.* p. 31.
9.   *Ibid.* p.33.
10. MacWhite Archives, a coded cablegram to Department of Foreign Affairs.
11. Katz, op. cit., p. 84.
12. Katz, op. cit., p.109. Items in square brackets added by cryptographer.
13. St Luke, op. cit., pp. 38–9.

Chapter 5

1.   Derry, op. cit., p. 33.
2.   *Ibid.* pp. 38–9.
3.   *Ibid.* p. 41.
4.   *Ibid.* pp. 49–50.
5.   *Ibid.* pp. 53–4.
6.   *Ibid.* p. 56.
7.   *Ibid.* p. 60.
8.   *Ibid.* p. 62.
9.   Sam Derry with David MacDonald, 'Vatican Pimpernel', *Reader's Digest*, November 1975.

Chapter 6

1.   O'Hara, op. cit., p. 115.
2.   *Ibid.* p. 118.
3.   *Ibid.* p. 119.
4.   National Archives Department of Foreign Affairs papers.
5.   Derry, op. cit., p. 64.
6.   *Ibid.* p. 71.
7.   Interview with Frank Lewis for his *Saturday Supplement* Programme on Radio Kerry, 11 June 1994.
8.   Bill Simpson, *A Vatican Lifeline '44*, p. 47.
9.   *Ibid.* p. 52.
10. John Furman, *Be not Fearful*, p. 93.
11. Gallagher, op. cit., p. 107.
12. The National Archives (UK), War Office Papers.

Chapter 7

1. Simpson, op. cit., pp. 60–1.
2. *Ibid.* p. 62.
3. Furman, John, op. cit., pp. 96–7.
4. E. Garrad-Cole, *Single to Rome*, p. 9.
5. *Ibid.* p. 13.
6. *Ibid.* p. 18.
7. *Ibid.* pp. 89, 90.
8. *Ibid.* p. 103.
9. *Ibid.* p. 104.
10. *Ibid.* p. 104.
11. Katz, R. op. cit., p. 128.
12. Sermoneta, op. cit., p. 224.
13. National Archives, Department of Foreign Affairs papers.
14. *Ibid.*
15. St Luke, op. cit., pp. 74–5.
16. Simpson, op. cit., p. 75.
17. *Ibid.* p. 76.
18. Furman, op. cit., p. 108.
19. *Ibid.* p. 109.
20. MacWhite Archives, a coded cablegram to Department of Foreign Affairs.
21. *Ibid.*
22. The National Archives (UK), War Office Papers.

Chapter 8

1. Simpson, op. cit., p. 81.
2. *Ibid.* p. 82.
3. Garrad-Cole, op. cit., pp. 86–8.
4. Derry, op. cit., p. 97.
5. Furman, op. cit., pp. 124–5.
6. *Ibid.* p. 125.
7. *Ibid.* p. 126.
8. D'Arcy Mander, *Mander's March on Rome*, p. 104.
9. *Ibid.* p. 105.
10. Simpson, op. cit., p. 92.
11. *Ibid.* p. 92.

12. Gallagher, op. cit., pp. 117–8.
13. *Ibid.* p. 117.
14. *Ibid.* p. 116.
15. Ibid. p. 117.
16. Derry, op. cit., pp. 108–9.

Chapter 9

1. Simpson, op. cit., pp. 124–5.
2. *Ibid.* p. 104.
3. Derry, op. cit., p. 115.
4. The National Archives (UK), War Office Papers.
5. Gallagher, op. cit., p. 120.
6. Simpson, op. cit., p. 137.
7. *Ibid.* p. 138.
8. Derry, op. cit., p. 153.
9. St Luke, op. cit., p. 101.
10. *Ibid.* p. 94.
11. Sermoneta, op. cit., p. 235.
12. Paul Freyberg, *Bernard Freyberg, VC: Soldier of Two Nations*, p. 454.
13. MacWhite Archives, a diary entry.
14. MacWhite Archives, a coded cablegram to Department of Foreign Affairs
15. Roy Jenkins, *Churchill* p. 729.
16. The National Archives (UK), War Office Papers.

Chapter 10

1. Furman, op. cit., p. 140.
2. O'Hara, op. cit., p. 107
3. Kiernan, op. cit., p. 48.
4. Furman, op. cit., p. 174.
5. *Ibid.* p. 175.
6. Derry, op. cit., p. 130.
7. *Ibid.* p. 141.
8. Freyberg, op. cit., p. 40.
9. Furman, op. cit., p. 187.
10. MacWhite Archives, a diary entry.
11. William Newnan, *Escape in Italy*, p. 39.
12. Gallagher, op. cit., p. 146.

13.   *Ibid.* p.13.

Chapter 11

1.   Garrad-Cole, op. cit., p.112.
2.   *Ibid.* pp. 113–4.
3.   *Ibid.* p. 115.
4.   *Ibid.* p. 117.
5.   Katz, op. cit., p. 234–5.
6.   Katz, op. cit., p. 226.
7.   St Luke, op. cit., p. 145.
8.   MacWhite Archives, a diary entry.
9.   Katz, op. cit., p. 274.
10.   In conversation with the author, 2007.
11.   The National Archives (UK), War Office Papers.
12.   The National Archives (UK), War Office Papers.
13.   Furman, op. cit., p. 111.
14.   Simpson, op. cit., p. 168.
15.   MacWhite Archives, a letter to the Department of Foreign Affairs. The Battle of Actium took place in 31 BC.
16.   St Luke, op. cit., p. 167.
17.   *Ibid.* p. 171.
18.   *Ibid.* p. 171.
19.   *Ibid.* pp. 171–2.
20.   The National Archives (UK), War Office Papers.

Chapter 12

1.   MacWhite Archives, a diary entry.
2.   Furman, op. cit., p. 206.
3.   St Luke, op. cit., p. 173.
4.   St Luke, op. cit., p. 174.
5.   MacWhite Archives, a diary entry.
6.   St Luke, op. cit., p. 178.
7.   Furman, op. cit., p. 208.
8.   *Ibid.* p. 103.
9.   The National Archives (UK), War Office Papers.
10.   Furman, op. cit., p. 209.
11.   *Ibid.* p. 209.
12.   *Ibid.* p. 209.

13.   *Ibid.* p. 211.
14.   St Luke, op. cit., p. 180.
15.   *Ibid.* p. 184.
16.   *Ibid.* p. 187.
17.   MacWhite Archives, a diary entry.
18.   Furman, op. cit., p. 214.
19.   St Luke, op. cit., pp. 189-90.
20.   *Ibid.* p. 192.
21.   *Ibid.* p. 192.
22.   Gallagher, op. cit., p. 171.
23.   *Ibid.* p. 171.
24.   *Ibid.* p. 171.
25.   Furman, op. cit., p. 218.
26.   St Luke, op. cit., p. 195.
27.   Katz, op. cit., p. 311.
28.   St Luke, op. cit., pp. 200–1.
29.   Harold Tittmann, *Inside the Vatican of Pius XII*, p. 210.
30.   Furman, op. cit., p. 221.
31.   Denis Johnston, *Nine Rivers from Jordan.* p. 251.
32.   *Ibid.* p. 253.
33.   *Ibid.* p. 250.

Chapter 13

1.   Johnston, op. cit., pp. 249–253.
2.   Kiernan, op. cit., p. 46.
3.   Interview with Frank Lewis for his *Saturday Supplement* Programme on Radio Kerry 11 June 1994.
4.   In correspondence with the author, 2007.
5.   *Ibid.*
6.   *Ibid.*
7.   Sam Derry, interview with Frank Lewis.
8.   Sam Derry with David MacDonald, 'Vatican Pimpernel', *Reader's Digest,* November 1975.
9.   *The New York Times*, 31 October 1963.
10.   O'Flaherty family archive.
11.   Sam Derry with David MacDonald, 'Vatican Pimpernel', *Reader's Digest*, November 1975.

12. In conversation with the author, 2007.
13. *Ibid.*
14. *Ibid.*
15. *Ibid.*
16. National Archives, Department of Foreign Affairs Papers.
17. *Ibid.*
18. Sermoneta, op. cit., p. 261.
19. In conversation with the author, 2007.
20. *Ibid.*
21. *Ibid.*
22. *Ibid.*

Chapter 14

1. National Archives, Department of Foreign Affairs Papers.
2. Fr Leonard Boyle interviewed by Maurice O'Keeffe in January 2004; CD no. 65 in his Irish Life and Lore, Kerry Collection.
3. Tittmann, op. cit., p. 97.
4. *Ibid.* p. 189.
5. R. Trevelyan, *Rome '44; The Battle for the Eternal City*, p. 16.
6. Furman, op. cit., p. 93.
7. In conversation with the author, 2007.
8. Sam Derry with David MacDonald, 'Vatican Pimpernel', *Reader's Digest*, November 1975.
9. *This is Your Life*, BBC broadcast February 1963.
10. *Ibid.*
11. *Ibid.*
12. *Ibid.*
13. Gallagher, op. cit., p. 184.
14. Interview with Frank Lewis for his *Saturday Supplement* Programme on Radio Kerry, 11 June 1994.
15. Fernande Leboucher, *The Incredible Mission of Fr Benoit*, p. 157.
16. O'Flaherty family archives.
17. M. Marchione, *Yours is a Precious Witness*, pp. 73–4.
18. Simpson, op. cit., p. iv.
19. Derry, op. cit., p. 4.
20. Hugh O'Flaherty, and John Smit, *O Roma Felix* p. 23.
21. In conversation with the author, 2007.

Sources

Books, articles

Absalom, Roger, *Hidden History, The Allies, The Resistance and Others in Occupied Italy 1943–1945*, The Historical Journal, 38(1), 1995.

Alexander, Harold, *The Alexander Memoirs*, London, Cassell, 1962.

Atkinson, Rick, *The Day of the Battle: The War in Sicily and Italy*, 1943–4, New York, Henry Holt and Co., 2007.

Chadwick, Owen, *Britain and the Vatican during the Second World War*, Cambridge, Cambridge University Press, 1986.

Dalin, Rabbi David G., *The Myth of Hitler's Pope*, Washington DC, Regnery Publishing, 2005.

D'Este, Carlo, *Eisenhower*, London, Cassell, 2004.

D'Este, Carlo, *Fatal Decision, Anzio and the Battle for Rome*, London, Aurum Press, 2007.

Derry, Sam with MacDonald, David, *Vatican Pimpernel*, Reader's Digest, November 1975.

Derry, Sam, *Rome Escape Line*, London, George Harrap, 1960.

Ellis, John, Cassino, *The Hollow Victory*, London, Aurum Press, 1984.

Freyberg, Paul, *Bernard Freyberg, VC.*, London, Hodder and Stoughton, 1991.

Furman, John, *Be Not Fearful*, New York, Roy Publishers, 1959.

Gallagher, J. P., *The Scarlet Pimpernel of the Vatican*, London, Souvenir Press, 1967.

Garrad-Cole, E., *Single to Rome*, London, Allan Wingate, 1955.

Hickey, Donal, *Queen of them All, a History of Killarney Golf and Fishing Club, Killarney*, Killarney Golf and Fishing Club, 1993.

Jenkins, Roy, *Churchill*, London, Macmillan, 2001.

Johnson, Denis, *Nine Rivers from Jordan*, London, Derek Verschoyle, 1953.

Katz, R., *Fatal Silence*, London, Weidenfeld and Nicholson, 2003.

Keegan, John, *The Second World War*, London, Pimlico, 1989.

Keogh, Dermot and O'Driscoll, Mervyn (eds.), *Ireland in World War II*, Cork, Mercier Press, 2004.

Kershaw, Ian, *Fateful Choices*, London, Allen Lane, 2007.

Kiernan, T. J. *Pope Pius XII*, Dublin, Clonmore and Reynolds, 1958.

Leboucher, Fernande, *The Incredible Mission of Fr. Benoit*, London, William Kimber, 1969.

MacGregor Burns, *James, Roosevelt, Vol. 1*, New York, Harcourt, Brace and World, 1956.

MacGregor Burns, *James, Roosevelt, Vol. 2*, New York, Harcourt, Brace and Jovanovich, 1956.

Madden, Daniel, *Operation Escape*, New York, Hawthorn Books, 1962.

Mander, D'Arcy, *Mander's March on Rome*, London, Allan Sutton, 1987.

Marchione, Margherita, *Yours is a Precious Witness*, New Jersey, Paulist Press, 1997.

Moseley, Ray, *The Last Days of Mussolini*, Gloucestershire, Sutton Publishing, 2004.

Muggeridge, Malcolm (ed.), *Ciano's Diary, 1937–8*, London, Methuen and Co., 1952.

Muggeridge, Malcolm (ed.), *Ciano's Diary, 1939–43*, London, Methuen and Co., 1947.

Newnan, William, *Escape in Italy*, Michigan, University of Michigan Press, 1945.

O'Flaherty, Hugh and Smit, John, *O Roma Felix*, Rome, Enrico Verdesi, 1949.

O'Hara, Aidan, *I'll live till I die: The Story of Delia Murphy*, Manorhamilton, Drumlin Publications, 1997.

O'Shea, Kieran, (ed.), *The Diocese of Kerry, formerly Ardfert*, Strasbourg, Éditions du Signe, 2005.

Portelli, Alessandro, *The Order Has Been Carried Out*, Hampshire, Palgrave Macmillan, 2003.

Rhodes, Anthony, *The Vatican in the Age of Dictators*, London, Hodder and Stoughton, 1973.

St Luke, Mother Mary (published under the pseudonym Jane Scrivener)

Inside Rome with the Germans, New York, The Macmillan Company, 1945.

Sermoneta, The Duchess of, *Sparkle Distant Worlds*, London, Hutchinson and Co., 1947.

Shirer, William, L., *The Rise and Fall of the Third Reich*, London, Arrow Books, 1960.

Simpson, Bill, *A Vatican Lifeline '44*, London, Leo Cooper, 1995.

Tittmann, Harold, *Inside the Vatican of Pius XII*, New York, Doubleday, 2004.

Tompkins, Peter, *A Spy in Rome*, London, Weidenfeld and Nicholson, 1962.

Trevelyan, Raleigh, *Rome ' 44*, London, Pimlico, 1981.

Tudor, Malcolm, *Escape from Italy, 1943–45*, Powys, Emilia Publishing, 2003.

Archives

The Department of Foreign Affairs Papers in the National Archives, Dublin.

The Papers of the late Michael MacWhite in the Archives Section of the James Joyce Library, University College Dublin.

The Activities of the British Organisation in Rome for assisting Allied escaped prisoners of war in the Public Records Office, Kew, London.

Audio, TV

Lewis, Frank, *An Interview with Sam Derry, Fr Leonard Boyle, Fr Sean Quinlan and others*, *Saturday Supplement* Programme, 11 June 1994 for Radio Kerry.

O'Keeffe, Maurice, *An interview with Noreen Dennehy*, CD No. 65 in his Irish Life and Lore (Kerry Collection) Series, (www.irishlifeandlore.com).

O'Shannon, Cathal, *Ireland's Nazis*, Tile Films Productions.

This is Your Life, an audio recording of the programme on Sam Derry, London, BBC, 1963.

Index

Index

Index